Essential
Teaching Skills

Third Edition

Chris Kyriacou

First published in 1991 by Basil Blackwell Ltd
Reprinted in 1992 by Simon and Schuster Education
Reprinted in 1995 by Stanley Thornes (Publishers) Ltd
Second edition 1998
Reprinted in 2001 by Nelson Thornes Ltd

Third edition published in 2007 by:
Nelson Thornes Ltd
Delta Place
27 Bath Road
CHELTENHAM
GL53 7TH
United Kingdom

09 10 11 / 10 9 8 7 6 5 4 3 2

A catalogue record for this book is available from the British Library

ISBN 978 0 7487 8161 4

Illustrations by Clinton Banbury
Page make-up by Florence Production Ltd, Stoodleigh, Devon

Printed by Multivista Global Ltd

Contents

Preface

In this book I outline the teaching skills which are involved in effective teaching. The book is designed to meet the needs of student teachers and experienced teachers wishing to explore and develop their own practice. It will also be of use to those involved in helping others to develop teaching skills or with an interest in this topic generally.

I have been very gratified by the immense popularity of this book since it first appeared. This new (third) edition has been revised to take account of important developments in education policy classroom practice, the introduction of new professional standards for beginning and experienced teachers, and the move towards evidence based teaching. This revised text incorporates developments in personalised learning, assessment for learning, whole-class interactive teaching, ICT, inclusion, initial teacher training, continuing professional development, and the Every Child Matters agenda.

1 Developing your teaching skills

The essence of being an effective teacher lies in knowing what to do to foster pupils' learning and being able to do it. Effective teaching is primarily concerned with setting up a learning activity for each pupil which is successful in bringing about the type of learning the teacher intends. The difference between knowing what to do and being able to do it can be well illustrated by making an analogy with playing tennis. A player may know that in a particular situation a lob over the opponent's head is required, but whether that shot can be played successfully may be an entirely different matter! The player's skills involve three elements. First, the knowledge about possible types of shots; second, the decision-making involved in deciding that a lob is in fact the most appropriate shot required; and third, the action involved in executing that shot.

The nature of teaching skills

Successful teaching skills thus crucially involve knowledge, decision-making and action. This distinction between these three elements underpinning skills is extremely important, because skilful teaching is as much a thinking activity as it is observable actions. Developing your skills as a teacher therefore is as much about developing and extending your knowledge about the decision you may take in a particular situation as it is about the successful execution of the observable action.

You must develop your action skills

Almost all teachers during their initial training will spend some time observing experienced teachers, and increasing numbers of experienced teachers now spend some time observing colleagues as part of their own or their colleagues' programme of professional development. Such observation can be immensely valuable; seeing how another teacher performs can stimulate your own ideas about your teaching. It may do this simply by acting as a model, either good or bad (seeing a colleague use an exceptionally well-prepared worksheet or one containing some obvious shortcomings may both stimulate your thinking about your own use of worksheets). Equally well, and more frequently, observation is stimulating because of the creative tension caused by trying to match your own decision-making about teaching with the decisions you infer your colleague has made. For example, you may normally go over some key points regarding why an experimental design used might be suspect, with the class as a whole, only to see a colleague using small group discussion instead. As a result, you may be stimulated to think about the reasons for this. Indeed, the benefits of classroom observation are greatly enhanced by having some time available before and after the lesson for discussion about the teaching.

The features of teaching skills

Over the years, much has been written about classroom teaching skills. The impetus for this has included those concerned with the initial training and the in-service training of teachers, those concerned to monitor the standard and quality of teaching performance, those involved in schemes of teacher appraisal, and those concerned with understanding, as a research endeavour, what constitutes successful teaching. As such, there is now a massive literature available for study. Overall, it appears that teaching skills can usefully be considered in terms of three key features:

- They involve purposeful and goal-directed behaviour.
- Their level of expertise is evidenced by the display of precision, smoothness and sensitivity to context.
- They can be improved by training and practice.

Studies of teaching skills

Studies of teaching skills have typically focused on how such skills are developed and displayed by beginning teachers and how beginning teachers differ from experienced teachers (Wragg, 2005). Wragg sees teaching skills as strategies that teachers use which facilitate pupils' learning and which are acknowledged by those competent to judge as being skills. Wragg also argues that the skill should be capable of being repeated. He further points out that focusing on particular skills in isolation can be unhelpful because they can become less meaningful out of context. Wragg believes that it is better to analyse particular skills in relation to broad areas of activity, such as class management, questioning and explaining.

Teachers' thinking

As well as studies focusing on developing skills amongst student teachers, a number of writers have focused on studying what experienced teachers think about the skills they use in teaching (Day, 2004; Pollard *et al.,* 2005). Such studies have viewed teaching as a complex cognitive skill, based on knowledge about how to construct and conduct a lesson, and knowledge about the content to be taught. This skill enables the teacher to construct lesson plans and make rapid decisions in the light of changing circumstances. The difference between novice teachers and experienced teachers is that the latter have developed sets of well-organised actions that they can apply flexibly and adapt with little mental effort to suit the situation.

A useful analogy here is that of going to a restaurant. Once you have been to several types of restaurant, you develop knowledge about the procedure that generally operates: whether you find a table or are shown to one; how to order from a menu; and when and how you pay. Such experience enables you to go to a new restaurant and cope with getting what you want reasonably skilfully. For someone who has never been to a restaurant, few sets of organised actions have been built up. For all the person may know, you may have to go to the kitchen, select some meat, and cook it yourself! Similarly, experienced teachers have built up a repertoire of many sets of behaviours from which to select that behaviour most appropriate to the immediate demands of the situation, whether it is dealing with a pupil who is unable to answer a question, or noticing a pupil looking out of a window. Indeed, the reason why teaching is so demanding in the early years is because new teachers have to build up their expertise of knowing what to do and being able to do it.

A number of writers have pointed out that a particular feature of teaching skills is their interactive nature. A teacher's actions during a lesson continuously need to take account of changing circumstances, many of which may be unexpected. Indeed, a teacher's effectiveness in the classroom is very dependent on how well they can modify and adapt their actions in the light of how well the lesson is going. In this sense, teaching is more like driving which involves negotiating a series of busy roundabouts than it is like driving along a quiet motorway. With experience, much of this interactive decision-making gradually becomes routine so that the teacher is hardly aware at a conscious level of the many decisions they are making during a lesson. In contrast, for a novice teacher, each new demand seems to require careful attention and thought.

Teachers' knowledge about teaching

Another important feature of teaching skills is that they clearly draw upon the teachers' knowledge about effective teaching (Campbell *et al.,* 2004; Muijs and Reynolds, 2005). Shulman (1987) famously argued that at the very least this knowledge base includes:

- knowledge about content
- knowledge about broad principles and strategies of classroom management and organisation
- knowledge about curriculum materials and programmes
- knowledge about the teaching of particular content topics
- knowledge about pupils
- knowledge about educational contexts, ranging from the classroom group to aspects of the community
- knowledge about educational aims and values.

For Shulman, teaching skills are bound up with teachers' thinking which draws upon their knowledge base as a basis for judgement and action.

This notion that as much emphasis in considering teaching skills must be given to the knowledge base as to the decision-making process, may seem odd, since clearly all decision-making must draw on teachers' knowledge about teaching. The basic point here is that such knowledge is largely implicit and taken for granted. However, if one is concerned with how teachers develop their teaching skills, this knowledge base needs to be made more explicit. A very effective way of doing this is to show teachers a video of their teaching and probe their thinking about what they did and why through this 'stimulated recall' method. This approach essentially tries to re-create the teacher's thinking in progress while they were actually teaching (often referred to as 'reflection-in-action').

A number of researchers have argued that in order to explore the teacher's knowledge base it is important to use a range of methods, such as in-depth interview, classroom observation, stimulated recall, and task analysis, in order to probe as clearly as possible the teacher's thinking that underpins their classroom decision-making.

Mentoring

Writings and studies looking at school mentors and their role in the professional development of student teachers and newly qualified teachers have also served to highlight the key skills that need to be developed in the early years of teaching (Robins, 2006; Stephens, 1996). Indeed, the increasingly important role played by mentors in schools during initial teacher training has indicated how turning effective teachers into effective trainers of new teachers is not unproblematic. A teacher may know how to teach well, but that may not translate easily into the role of how best to guide and help student teachers develop their own expertise. Writings and studies looking at effective mentoring have thus attempted to highlight the key skills involved in teaching and to explore how mentors can best foster such skills amongst beginning teachers.

Defining essential teaching skills

Teaching skills can be defined as discrete and coherent activities by teachers which foster pupil learning. In the light of our consideration of teaching skills so far in this chapter, three important elements of skills are discernible:

- *Knowledge,* comprising the teacher's knowledge about the subject, pupils, curriculum, teaching methods, the influence on teaching and learning of other factors, and knowledge about one's own teaching skills.
- *Decision-making,* comprising the thinking and decision-making that occurs before, during and after a lesson, concerning how best to achieve the educational outcomes intended.
- *Action,* comprising the overt behaviour by teachers undertaken to foster pupil learning.

An over-riding feature of teaching skills is that they are purposeful and goal-directed activities which are essentially problem-solving. At its broadest, the problem is how best to deliver effectively the educational outcomes, in terms of pupil learning, required. More specifically, teaching skills are concerned with all the short-term and immediate problems faced before, during and after the lesson, such as 'How can I lay out the key points of this topic in a PowerPoint presentation?', 'How can I signal to a pupil to stop talking without interrupting what I am explaining to the whole class?', 'What can I write when assessing a piece of work by a pupil to highlight a flaw in the pupil's argument?'.

Teaching skills are also concerned with the long-term problems of effective teaching, such as 'Which textbook series best meets the needs of my pupils?', 'How best can I update my subject knowledge?', 'How do I best prepare pupils for the work they will be doing in future years?'.

Identifying essential teaching skills

One of the major problems in trying to identify a list of essential teaching skills is that teaching skills vary from very broad and general skills, such as the planning of lessons, to very specific skills, such as the appropriate length of time to wait for a pupil to answer a question in a particular type of situation. Overall, in considering teaching skills, it seems to be most useful to focus on fairly broad and general skills which are meaningful to teachers and relate to how they think about their teaching. More specific skills can then be discussed as and when they help illustrate and illuminate how these general skills operate. Nevertheless, given the nature of teaching, it is clear that whatever set of general skills is chosen to focus on, the overlap and interplay between them will be marked, and a good case can always be made by others for focusing on a different set. For example, Hay McBer (2000) identified the following list of teaching skills:

- high expectations
- planning
- methods and strategies
- pupil management/discipline
- time and resource management
- assessment
- homework.

Over the years there has been a wealth of writing about and use of lists of teaching skills, both by those involved in teacher education and by educational researchers. There is no definitively agreed list. A consideration of the various writings, however, indicates that a fairly typical list of teaching skills can be identified. Such lists of teaching skills have proved to be very useful in helping both beginning and experienced teachers to think about and develop their classroom practice.

The effective teacher

Writings on the notion of the effective teacher have also yielded a mass of material on the skills displayed by teachers considered to be effective (Campbell *et al.,* 2004; Kerry and Wilding, 2004; Kyriacou, 1997; Muijs and Reynolds, 2005). Teachers judged to be effective appear to display the following skills in their teaching:

- establishing an orderly and attractive learning environment
- concentrating on teaching and learning by maximising learning time and maintaining an academic emphasis
- purposeful teaching through the use of well-organised and well-structured lessons coupled with clarity of purpose
- conveying high expectations and providing intellectual challenge
- monitoring progress and providing quick corrective feedback
- establishing clear and fair discipline.

Teacher appraisal and performance review

Another important source of information about teaching skills can be found in the wealth of material dealing with the appraisal and performance review of established teachers (Jones *et al.,* 2006; Middlewood and Cardno, 2001). These include a whole host of lesson observation schedules and rating scales used to identify and comment on the extent to which teaching skills are displayed in the lessons observed. Such writings and schedules typically focus on areas such as:

- *Preparation and planning:* e.g. selects short-term objectives related to the school's curriculum guidelines, and is aware of and uses, as and when appropriate, a variety of equipment and resources.
- *Classroom organisation and management:* e.g. uses time and space to maximum advantage and ensures smooth transitions from one activity to another.
- *Communication skills:* e.g. uses questioning and explaining effectively.
- *The setting of work for pupils:* e.g. work is appropriate for age and ability, is of sound quality, and displays fitness for purpose.
- *Assessment of pupils' work and record keeping:* e.g. provides feedback to pupils that helps them improve their work in future.
- *Knowledge of relevant subject matter:* e.g. uses a knowledge of the topic to develop and guide pupils towards a secure base of understanding.
- *Relationships with pupils:* e.g. shows a genuine interest in and respect for children's words and thoughts and focuses on children's behaviour rather than personality.

Skills identified by the DfES

The Department for Education and Skills (DfES) has increasingly been involved in drawing attention to the teaching skills underpinning good classroom practice in both primary and secondary schools, and these have featured heavily in support materials and training to help teachers to adopt the type of classroom practice advocated by the DfES in delivering various national strategies (e.g. DfES, 2003a, 2003b, 2004a). The DfES (2004a) in its consideration of teaching in secondary schools produced a training pack dealing with teaching skills in the following areas:

- Designing lessons
  - structured learning
  - teaching models
  - lesson design for lower attainers
  - lesson design for inclusion
  - starters and plenaries
- Teaching repertoire
  - modelling
  - questioning
  - explaining
  - guided learning
  - group work
  - active engagement techniques
- Creating effective learners
  - assessment for learning
  - developing reading
  - developing writing
  - using ICT to enhance learning
  - leading in learning
  - developing effective learning
- Creating conditions for learning
  - improving the climate for learning
  - learning styles.

Packs dealing with teaching skills, such as these, can be downloaded free of charge from the DfES website (www.dfes.gov.uk).

Qualities looked for by Ofsted

For many years Her Majesty's Inspectorate (HMI) and the Office for Standards in Education (Ofsted) have published reports dealing with the quality of teaching observed during their inspections of schools. This includes an annual report on standards in education, the publication of handbooks and other support materials used by inspectors in their inspection of schools, and also the findings of reports focusing on specific subjects, levels and topics, and on specific aspects of teaching, such as the quality of teaching displayed by newly qualified teachers and the quality of teaching experienced by particular groups of pupils (e.g. Ofsted, 2002, 2006). From these reports one is able to build up a clear picture of the types of skills school inspectors expect to see displayed when good teaching is taking place. These can be inferred from the following descriptions commonly used by Ofsted:

- Lessons should be purposeful with high expectations conveyed.
- Pupils should be given some opportunities to organise their own work (over-direction by teachers needs to be guarded against).

- Lessons should elicit and sustain pupils' interest and be perceived by pupils as relevant and challenging.
- The work should be well matched to pupils' abilities and learning needs.
- Pupils' language should be developed and extended (teachers' questioning skills play a part here).
- A variety of learning activities should be employed.
- Good order and control should be largely based on skilful management of pupils' involvement in the lesson, and mutual respect.

The teaching skills looked for by Ofsted are modified from time to time to take account of new DfES policies. For example, the introduction by the DfES (2004b) of the Every Child Matters agenda led to a revision of Ofsted's lesson observation schedule so that it was 'aligned' with those teaching skills which related to this agenda (Cheminais, 2006). This agenda views pupil performance and pupil well-being as going hand in hand, and identifies five outcomes for children:

- *Being healthy:* helping pupils to adopt healthy lifestyles, build their self-esteem, eat and drink well and lead active lives.
- *Staying safe:* keeping pupils safe from bullying, harassment and other dangers.
- *Enjoying and achieving:* enabling pupils to make good progress in their work and personal development and to enjoy their education.
- *Making a positive contribution:* ensuring that pupils understand their rights and responsibilities, are listened to, and participate in the life of the community.
- *Achieving social and economic well-being:* helping pupils to gain the skills and knowledge needed for future employment.

In the revised form, a lesson graded as outstanding included the following characteristics:

- Excellent relationships are most conducive to pupils' personal development.
- All pupils are challenged and stretched whatever standard they are working at.
- Assessment of pupils' work successfully underpins the teaching and pupils have a clear idea of how to improve.

Skills to be developed during initial training and beyond

A further source of information relating to teaching skills comes from writings and materials concerned with the teaching skills that student teachers are expected to develop during their initial teacher training (Stephens and Crawley, 1994; Training and Development Agency for Schools (TDA), 2007). These include a variety of profiling documents developed by teacher training institutions to help foster and record student teachers' progress in developing teaching skills over the course of their training. A study by Hobson *et al.* (2006) asked student teachers to rate the importance of eight different types of knowledge and skills that beginning teachers needed to develop. The student teachers' ratings of these in order of importance were:

- ability to bring about pupil learning
- ability to maintain discipline in the classroom

- ability to use a range of teaching methods
- knowledge about their teaching subject(s)
- ability to deal with pastoral issues
- staff supervision/management skills
- knowledge/understanding of education policy
- awareness of research findings about effective teaching methods.

Of particular significance in this respect is the attempt by government agencies to specify the list of skills to be developed. For example, the TDA (2007) published a list of professional standards that primary and secondary school student teachers in England and Wales need to have acquired in order to be awarded Qualified Teacher Status (QTS) from September 2007. The QTS standards are grouped into three areas:

- Professional attributes
  - relationships with children and young people
  - frameworks
  - communicating and working with others
  - personal professional development
- Professional knowledge and understanding
  - teaching and learning
  - assessment and monitoring
  - subjects and curriculum
  - literacy, numeracy and ICT
  - achievement and diversity
  - health and well-being
- Professional skills
  - planning
  - teaching
  - assessing, monitoring and giving feedback
  - reviewing teaching and learning
  - learning environment
  - team working and collaboration.

The QTS standards are used by the TDA and Ofsted to monitor the quality and effectiveness of initial teacher training courses. This list will undoubtedly be modified from time to time. Indeed, the above list superseded lists drawn up earlier. Parts of the specific criteria within each area are worded the same for both primary and secondary teachers, whilst some parts are worded differently. Overall, however, an attempt has been made to use, as far as possible, the same form of words to describe the standards expected of both primary and secondary school teachers.

A similar list of standards has also been drawn up to set out the teaching skills that newly qualified teachers are expected to display during their first year (the induction year). Newly qualified teachers are required to achieve these induction standards in order to have their QTS ratified. The induction standards require newly qualified teachers to continue to meet the QTS standards, but to add to these some areas of enhancement.

Three further lists of standards have been drawn up by the DfES to cover the teaching skills (and other work) expected of more experienced teachers. These are:

- the threshold standards
- the advanced skills teacher standards
- the excellent teacher standards.

Looking at the description of the teaching skills associated with these three sets of standards (compared with the QTS standards and the induction standards) there is much greater emphasis here on evidence that their teaching produces higher pupil attainment, on their awareness of what constitutes best classroom practice, and on their ability to develop the practice of colleagues.

Evidence-based classroom practice

Another set of increasing literature on teaching skills comes from the attempts to provide an evidence base to inform developments in policy and practice in education (Thomas and Pring, 2004; Petty, 2006). This approach includes both original research studies (such as DfES research reports) and systematic reviews which look at the existing research literature on a particular topic; they also synthesise the research evidence in order to assess what impact different types of teaching approaches and intervention strategies have on pupils' learning. Such research often highlights particular aspects of teaching skills that are crucial in determining the extent to which a particular approach has had a positive impact on pupils' learning. For example, a systematic review looking at the impact of daily mathematics lessons (the numeracy hour), introduced as part of the National Numeracy Strategy in primary schools, highlighted the need for many teachers to develop the skills necessary to sustain the 'interactive' aspect of whole-class 'interactive' teaching that was advocated in the National Numeracy Strategy (Kyriacou, 2005).

In the USA, a number of authors have a used synthesis of the evidence-base for 'what works' to identify the key sets of teaching skills. For example, an analysis by Stronge (2002) identified five sets of key teaching skills:

- the teacher as a person
- the teacher as classroom manager and organiser
- organising for instruction
- implementing instruction
- the teacher teaching: monitoring pupil progress and potential.

In contrast, another analysis in the USA, by Marzano (2003), identified three sets of key skills:

- instructional strategies
- classroom management
- classroom curriculum design.

Both Stronge (2002) and Marzano (2003), however, illustrate how the expert teacher differs from the beginning (novice) teacher in the extent to which they display a high level of these skills.

A list of essential teaching skills

Overall, the essential teaching skills involved in contributing to successful classroom practice can be identified and described as follows:

- *Planning and preparation:* the skills involved in selecting the educational aims and learning outcomes intended for a lesson and how best to achieve these.
- *Lesson presentation:* the skills involved in successfully engaging pupils in the learning experience, particularly in relation to the quality of instruction.
- *Lesson management:* the skills involved in managing and organising the learning activities taking place during the lesson to maintain pupils' attention, interest and involvement.
- *Classroom climate:* the skills involved in establishing and maintaining positive attitudes and motivation by pupils towards the lesson.
- *Discipline:* the skills involved in maintaining good order and dealing with any pupil misbehaviour that occurs.
- *Assessing pupils' progress:* the skills involved in assessing pupils' progress, covering both formative (i.e. intended to aid pupils' further development) and summative (i.e. providing a record of attainment) purposes of assessment.
- *Reflection and evaluation:* the skills involved in evaluating one's own current teaching practice in order to improve future practice.

These seven sets of essential teaching skills are further developed in Table 1, and form the basis for each of the following chapters of this book.

Two important points, however, need to be borne in mind when considering these skills. First, there is clearly an interplay between these seven areas, so that the skills exercised in one area may simultaneously contribute to another area. For example, smooth transition between activities is included within lesson management, but at the same time will also contribute to maintaining discipline. Second, all the skills involved in lesson presentation, lesson management, classroom climate and discipline, are interactive skills. In other words, exercising these skills involves monitoring, adjusting and responding to what pupils are doing. Unlike acting on a stage, where one can perform without an audience, these skills cannot be displayed in isolation from their interaction with pupils' behaviour. Even when giving an explanation, for example, a teacher would, at the very least, be attentive to the faces of pupils to judge whether it was being pitched appropriately for their needs, and might elaborate, alter the pace of delivery, tone of voice, content, or even stop and ask a question, in the light of what the facial expressions indicated.

The development of teaching skills

In defining teaching skills earlier, three elements were highlighted: knowledge, decision-making and action. Almost all beginning teachers will have had much experience of being taught as pupils themselves in a school. Without doubt, this will be the single most important influence on their knowledge about teaching and the models

Table 1 Essential teaching skills

Planning and preparation
- The lesson plan has clear and suitable aims and objectives.
- The content, methods and structure of the lesson selected are appropriate for the pupil learning intended.
- The lesson is planned to link up appropriately with past and future lessons.
- Materials, resources and aids are well prepared and checked in good time.
- All planning decisions take account of the pupils and the context.
- The lesson is designed to elicit and sustain pupils' attention, interest and involvement.

Lesson presentation
- The teacher's manner is confident, relaxed, self-assured and purposeful, and generates interest in the lesson.
- The teacher's instructions and explanations are clear and matched to pupils' needs.
- The teacher's questions include a variety of types and range and are distributed widely.
- A variety of appropriate learning activities are used to foster pupil learning.
- Pupils are actively involved in the lesson and are given opportunities to organise their own work.
- The teacher shows respect and encouragement for pupils' ideas and contributions, and fosters their development.
- The work undertaken by pupils is well matched to their needs.
- Materials, resources and aids are used to good effect.

Lesson management
- The beginning of the lesson is smooth and prompt, and sets up a positive mental set for what is to follow.
- Pupils' attention, interest and involvement in the lesson are maintained.
- Pupils' progress during the lesson is carefully monitored.
- Constructive and helpful feedback is given to pupils to encourage further progress.
- Transitions between activities are smooth.
- The time spent on different activities is well managed.
- The pace and flow of the lesson is adjusted and maintained at an appropriate level throughout the lesson.
- Adjustments to the lesson plan are made whenever appropriate.
- The ending of the lesson is used to good effect.

Classroom climate
- The climate is purposeful, task-oriented, relaxed, and with an established sense of order.
- Pupils are supported and encouraged to learn, with high expectations conveyed by the teacher.
- Teacher–pupil relationships are largely based on mutual respect and rapport.
- Feedback from the teacher contributes to fostering pupil self-confidence and self-esteem.
- The appearance and layout of the class are conducive to positive pupil attitudes towards the lesson and facilitate the activities taking place.

Discipline

- Good order is largely based on the positive classroom climate established and on good lesson presentation and management.
- The teacher's authority is established and accepted by pupils.
- Clear rules and expectations regarding pupil behaviour are conveyed by the teacher at appropriate times.
- Pupil behaviour is carefully monitored and appropriate actions by the teacher are taken to pre-empt misbehaviour.
- Pupil misbehaviour is dealt with by an appropriate use of investigation, counselling, academic help, reprimands and punishments.
- Confrontations are avoided, and skilfully defused.

Assessing pupils' progress

- The marking of pupils' work during and after lessons is thorough and constructive, and work is returned in good time.
- Feedback on assessments aims not only to be diagnostic and corrective, but also to encourage further effort and maintain self-confidence, which involves follow-up comments, help or work with particular pupils as appropriate.
- A variety of assessment tasks are used, covering both formative and summative purposes.
- A variety of records of progress are kept.
- Some opportunities are given to foster pupils' own assessments of their work and progress.
- Assessment of pupils' work is used to identify areas of common difficulties, the effectiveness of the teaching, and whether a firm basis for further progress has been established.
- Assessment is made of the study skills and learning strategies employed by pupils in order to foster their further development.

Reflection and evaluation

- Lessons are evaluated to inform future planning and practice.
- Current practice is regularly considered with a view to identifying aspects for useful development.
- Use is made of a variety of ways to reflect upon and evaluate current practice.
- The teacher regularly reviews whether his or her time and effort can be organised to better effect.
- The teacher regularly reviews the strategies and techniques he or she uses to deal with sources of stress.

they have of how to conduct a lesson. Numerous studies, however, have indicated just how inadequate a base this is for attempting to teach one's first few lessons. Long experience of being taught certainly provides a broad framework for thinking about how to teach, but once the teacher's role is taken on, it becomes very evident that a whole range of teaching skills needs to be developed. For example, common problems experienced by beginning teachers include not knowing what to do when, having given an explanation, the pupil does not understand, other than repeating the same explanation; not knowing how to cope with pupils working at different rates, ranging from those who finish early to those making little progress; not knowing which curriculum elements require more attention and emphasis in teaching; and not knowing what to do with pupils they cannot control.

Some studies have explicitly compared beginning teachers (either student teachers or newly qualified teachers) with experienced teachers to highlight the development of teaching skills. These indicate that beginning teachers more often became engrossed in private exchanges with pupils so as to lose overall perception of what was going on elsewhere. Experienced teachers, on the other hand, are more able to split their attention between the pupil and the rest of the class, and can break off and comment on what is happening elsewhere, as and when appropriate. When it comes to planning lessons, experienced teachers are more selective in using the information provided by others, and prefer to rely on their knowledge of what they could typically expect from pupils of the age and class size given. In effect, the experienced teachers are able to use their repertoire of how to set up and deliver learning activities, which is largely denied or non-existent for beginning teachers.

Monitoring your own teaching

Another source of information about how teaching skills develop concerns the efforts of experienced teachers to monitor and develop their own skills or to assist with developing those of colleagues. Such work has taken place either as part of formal schemes of teacher appraisal and staff development or simply as part of the teacher's own concern to monitor and develop their own practice.

Of particular interest as an example of the latter, has been the growth of teacher action research (Costello, 2003; Koshy, 2005). This involves a systematic procedure in which teachers look at some aspect of their own or the school's practice that is giving rise to some concern, identify the precise nature of the problem, collect some data on the problem, and then devise, implement and evaluate a solution. Many teachers have used this approach to develop some aspect of their teaching skills, ranging from dealing with new approaches to teaching and learning (such as the use of more small group work) to simply improving skills that are already well developed (such as the quality of giving individual help). Studies reporting the efforts of experienced teachers to develop their teaching skills well illustrate that all teachers, not just beginning teachers, are continually involved in such development. Indeed, it is the sense that teaching skills continually need development to improve one's own practice and to meet new demands that makes teaching such a challenging profession.

Stages of development

Perrott (1982), in her analysis of how teaching skills are acquired and developed, focuses on three stages. The first stage is cognitive and involves developing an awareness, by study and observation, of what the skill is, identifying the various elements of the skill and their sequencing, knowing the purpose of using the skill, and knowing how it will benefit your teaching. She identifies the second stage as practice, normally in the classroom but occasionally in a controlled setting as part of a training course in which there is a short practice of a specific skill. The third stage is feedback, which enables the teacher to improve the performance of the skill by evaluating the relative success of its performance. Such feedback can range from simply an impressionistic sense of its successful performance to detailed feedback given by an observer, the use of audio-visual recording, or systematic data collected from pupils about their work, behaviour or opinions. Perrott sees this three-stage process as a cycle, in which the third stage feeds back into the first stage as part of an on-going development of the skill.

Having the ability to develop your skills

While it is clear that teachers are continually reflecting upon and developing their skills, it is also evident that this does not automatically lead to skilled performance. There are many teachers who, after years of experience, still have evident shortcomings in some teaching skills. In part, this reflects the fact that skilled performance also depends on ability and motivation. The teacher needs the ability to profit from reflection and practice, and the motivation to do so. If we consider questioning skills as an example, clearly all teachers need to develop such skills. However, while some teachers have built up great skills in the variety and range of question types they use and the skill with which they target pupils and elicit and elaborate pupils' responses, other experienced teachers may still show shortcomings in these respects. Why should this be so?

Earlier, I argued that skills involve knowledge, decision-making and action. All three of these elements are subject to the various general abilities of teachers. The teacher may simply not have built up the knowledge about the effective use of questioning skills, or have difficulty in making the appropriate decisions which use that knowledge, or have difficulties in carrying out the actions required in a skilled manner.

If we extend the example of questioning skills further, an example where the fault lies with inadequate knowledge would be a teacher who is simply unaware of the educational importance and benefits of using 'open' questions (questions where a number of correct answers are possible) as well as 'closed' questions (questions where only one correct answer is acceptable). An example where the fault lies with decision-making would be an inappropriate decision to simply repeat the same question to a pupil having a difficulty answering, rather than to phrase the question in a different way or perhaps provide a hint. An example where the fault lies in action would be a teacher who is unable to ask a question in a clear and unambiguous way. The relevant general abilities of the teacher involved here may not simply be intellectual ones, since much skilled performance depends on aspects of the teacher's personality or even acting ability. Some teachers find it easier than others to continually ask questions sounding

Practise your exposition

as though they are genuinely curious and interested in the replies, and comfortable with the longer pauses of silence required to give pupils time to think when being asked a more complex question.

Being motivated to develop your skills

Developing teaching skills also depends on the teacher's motivation. Teachers vary immensely in the extent to which they are prepared to invest time, energy and effort to reflect upon, evaluate and improve their teaching skills. This is particularly a problem once a teacher has developed a sufficiently adequate range of teaching skills to give satisfactory lessons. Teaching often then becomes a matter of routine. This can become even more confirmed once various materials, examples and strategies have been prepared and practised.

In addition, to some extent teachers' approaches to lessons tend to play to their own strengths. Thus, for example, a teacher who finds lessons generally work well if based on worksheets, close monitoring of progress, and one-to-one help, but in contrast finds lessons involving group work and class discussion tend to become noisy and chaotic, is more likely to design lessons based on the former than to develop and extend the skills involved in making the latter type of lessons successful. Indeed, one of the main reasons underlying the hostility against a particular curriculum innovation that may be felt by some teachers relates to the changes in their general approach and teaching skills required by the innovation. It says much for the professional commitment and sense of vocation of teachers, that the vast majority do spend much time and effort in continuing to develop their teaching skills and to develop new approaches to their teaching in the educational interests of their pupils.

Your professional development

It is also important to note that the responsibility to develop and extend your teaching skills is not simply your personal responsibility. Rather, it is also the responsibility of those within the school and agencies outside the school to ensure that such development is facilitated as part of your professional development, and as part of staff development at the school as a whole.

Mention has already been made of teacher appraisal and of the impetus that comes from curriculum innovation. Equally important, however, is the climate that exists within the school to facilitate the development of teaching skills as an ongoing process. An important part of school improvement and the capacity of the school for self-renewal is the ability of the school to create a positive climate which facilitates staff developing their teaching skills. The characteristics of schools that are particularly good at creating this type of positive climate tend to include the following:

- a sense of common ownership amongst staff for the educational aims to be achieved
- a constant generation of ideas
- sharing problems
- mutual support
- respect for each other's opinions
- an open and co-operative approach to dealing with conflicts and crises
- allowing styles to vary according to situations and needs
- encouraging anyone, not just leaders, to propose improvements
- an 'organic' rather than 'bureaucratic' management style (the former being more informal and flexible, with decision-making shared rather than directed from the top through a hierarchy, and with less emphasis on reports and record keeping).

Finally, it is worth bearing in mind that, despite the immense importance of developing sound teaching skills and seeing this as on ongoing process throughout your teaching career, teaching also involves a whole host of other important demands, both inside and outside the classroom. The reality of life as a teacher requires a prioritising and monitoring of the whole range of skills in doing your job effectively, and it will be both normal and sensible to find that skills other than those considered here will occasionally need attention. Perhaps it is best to view the development of your teaching skills as a process that is always in operation, but which varies in intensity depending on the situation and context you find yourself in. If your teaching is to retain the sharpness, freshness and cutting edge that characterises the most effective teaching, it is crucial that your skills are never allowed to rest for too long on the back burner.

Further reading

Campbell, J., Kyriakides, L., Muijs, D. and Robinson, W. (2004) *Assessing Teacher Effectiveness: Developing a Differentiated Model.* London: RoutledgeFalmer. This book looks at the research evidence on the nature of teacher effectiveness and how teaching skills need to take account of different contexts.

Day, C. (2004) *A Passion for Teaching*. London: RoutledgeFalmer. An insightful analysis of the work involved in being a successful teacher, which informs our understanding of teaching skills.

Kerry, T. and Wilding, M. (2004) *Effective Classroom Teacher: Developing the Skills You Need in Today's Classroom*. London: Pearson. An excellent overview of the facets involved in being an effective teacher and the teaching skills that underpin these.

Petty, G. (2006) *Evidence-Based Teaching: A Practical Approach*. Cheltenham: Nelson Thornes. An excellent analysis of effective teaching which draws upon research evidence concerning the effectiveness of different teaching methods.

2 Planning and preparation

The key task facing teachers is to set up a learning activity which effectively achieves the learning outcomes intended for each pupil. At the start of a lesson, all teachers need to have some idea of what learning they wish to take place and how the lesson will facilitate that learning. While student teachers on teaching practice are usually required to make explicit lesson plans, experienced teachers more often rely on their extensive experience to form a mental framework of how they want the lesson to proceed. This does not necessarily mean that the lesson plans of established teachers are any less detailed than those of beginning teachers, simply that the lesson plans have become internalised through repetition.

The elements of planning and preparation

Much has been written over the years about the planning and preparation of lessons (Butt, 2006; Skowron, 2006; Tileston, 2004). This has identified four major elements involved in planning a lesson:

- A *decision about the educational objectives* that the lesson will be designed to foster.
- A *selection and scripting of a lesson*, which involves deciding on the type and nature of the activities to be used (e.g. exposition, group work, reading), the order and timing of each of these activities, and the content and materials to be used.
- A *preparation of all the props to be used*, including materials, worked examples, checking that apparatus is ordered, delivered and in working order, arranging the layout of the classroom and, on occasion, even a rehearsal (such as when a new experiment or demonstration is involved).
- A *decision regarding how you will monitor and assess pupils' progress and attainment* during and after the lesson to evaluate whether the intended learning has taken place.

Meeting the needs of learners

Ofsted (1995, 2006), in their evaluation of lessons, typically focus on two crucial aspects in relation to planning and preparation. First, is it clear what the purpose of the lesson is? Second, has the lesson taken adequate account of the learners' needs? The former question addresses the question of how clearly specified the educational objectives of the lesson were. The latter question addresses the extent to which the educational objectives take adequate account of the range and type of pupils' abilities, their previous learning, and their progress towards future educational attainment.

It is perhaps the teacher's sensitivity to pupils' needs that is the most important of all the skills involved in effective teaching. This refers to the ability of the teacher to plan lessons and adapt and modify their delivery by taking account of how the lesson will be experienced by different pupils and foster their learning. It is impossible and meaningless to attempt to evaluate the quality of a lesson plan without taking into account how well it meets the needs of the pupils in the context in which it will take place.

Skills in planning

As noted in the previous chapter, an additional source of information concerning essential teaching skills comes from an examination of the attempt to list the skills that should be developed during a course of initial teaching training. For example, the TDA (2007) QTS standards include a number of elements on planning. These focus on:

- planning for progression across the age and ability range
- designing effective learning sequences within lessons and across a series of lessons
- designing opportunities for pupils to develop literacy, numeracy and ICT skills
- planning homework and other out-of-class work to sustain pupils' progress
- incorporating a range a teaching strategies and resources, including e-learning
- taking practical account of diversity and promoting equality and inclusion
- building upon pupils' prior knowledge.

Educational objectives

Selecting the educational objectives for a lesson is no mean task (Gronlund and Nivaldo, 2004). At the very least, they must contribute to broad educationally worthwhile aims. However, fashions change, and what is regarded as worthwhile at one time (e.g. rote memorisation of the ports around the British coastline) may now be considered inappropriate. Many schools list a number of educational aims in their prospectuses. The aims of the school's curriculum, as specified in the 1988 Education Reform Act, lay down an important framework. This states that the school's curriculum should:

- promote the spiritual, moral, cultural, mental and physical development of pupils at the school and of society
- prepare such pupils for the opportunities, responsibilities and experiences of adult life.

The Education Reform Act established a National Curriculum which specified the subjects that should be offered in the school curriculum, together with particular Attainment Targets that should be addressed during the pupils' school careers. Despite the great detail specified by the National Curriculum, this only provided a broad framework within which teachers still needed to plan individual lessons.

In selecting educational objectives, the teacher is obliged to specify clear learning outcomes which can usefully be analysed in terms of the development of pupils' knowledge, understanding, skills and attitudes. This planning is extremely complex, because a teacher inevitably has a range of outcomes in mind for a particular lesson, and indeed, the outcomes intended may differ markedly between the pupils in the class. In addition, all lessons involve an interplay between intellectual development (defined primarily in terms of a growth in pupils' knowledge, understanding and skills) and social development (defined primarily in terms of a growth in pupils' self-esteem and self-confidence in themselves as learners, an increased positive attitude towards the subject, and a greater maturity in their behaviour and interactions with others in the class). A teacher may thus have the development of an understanding of the concept of area as a major educational objective for a particular lesson. At the same time, there may be an overlay of other objectives in operation, such as the intention to give a particular able pupil the opportunity to do some extended work on this topic, the intention to help and encourage a pupil who has been showing a lack of interest, and the intention to use this topic to show that doing mathematics is fun and relates to important real-life applications. Only by being aware of such differing intentions can an observer make sense of the teacher's behaviour in the lesson.

Teachers' use of objectives in planning

While the notion of setting educational objectives is widely agreed to be an essential aspect of planning, some research on teachers' planning appears to indicate that many teachers do not start their planning of lessons by identifying educational objectives and then designing a lesson to deliver these objectives. Rather, they approach the task of planning in a more problem-solving manner by addressing the problem of how best to structure the time and experience of pupils during the lesson. This would suggest that many teachers may plan lessons without having clear learning outcomes in mind. I think, however, this is a misinterpretation based on the fact that if you ask a teacher to talk about their planning of a lesson, the educational objectives for the lesson are often left implicit, and greater attention is devoted to their description of the activities to be employed. Indeed, there is clear research evidence that teachers do think about educational objectives in planning their lessons, and that this is often made explicit by teachers when they talk about the thinking that occurs during and after the lesson. Overall, it appears that part of the problem in identifying how and when teachers specify the educational objectives for a lesson simply concerns how they articulate their thoughts to others.

The purposes and functions of planning

There are a number of important purposes and functions to the planning of lessons which are worth noting. First and foremost, it enables you to think clearly and specifically about the type of learning you wish to occur in a particular lesson, and to relate the educational objectives to what you know about the pupils and the place of the lesson in the general programme of study.

Second, it enables you to think about the structure and content of the lesson. This includes, most importantly, thinking about how long to devote to each activity. Indeed, one of the most important skills in teaching is that of judging how much time should be spent on each activity in a lesson and the best pace of progress through the activities.

Third, planning quite considerably reduces how much thinking you will have to do during the lesson. Once the lesson is in progress, there will be much to think about in order to maintain its effectiveness. The fact that the lesson as a whole has been well planned means that you can normally focus your attention on the fine-tuning of the lesson, rather than trying to make critical decisions on the hop. Indeed, many decisions about a lesson can only adequately be taken in advance. For example, if it becomes evident that a map is needed during a lesson, there may be little you can do about it if you had not realised this during your planning and had one available in case the need arose. A related point to this is that being under pressure is not a good state to be in when trying to make sensible decisions about teaching. You can all too easily find that trying to direct or alter the course of a lesson while teaching can lead to difficulties, until you have developed with experience a good sense of what will work and how, in the circumstances you face.

Fourth, planning leads on to the preparation of all the materials and resources in general that will be needed. For example, having some work already prepared for any pupils who might finish the intended work for the lesson well ahead of the majority, or a summary of some key points you wish to review between two activities, all enable the lesson to progress more smoothly and effectively.

A fifth important purpose of planning is that keeping your notes will provide a useful record for your future planning, particularly in relation to giving a similar lesson to another group of pupils and in your planning of future work with the pupils which will extend what they have done in that particular lesson. Indeed, it is very useful, particularly in the early years of teaching, to make a brief note at the end of each lesson of any point you want to draw to your attention at some future time when you need to refer to the lesson notes again.

Time spent planning

The amount of time spent planning also varies immensely between teachers and for the same teacher between lessons. While beginning teachers will certainly need to spend more time planning, some of the differences between teachers at the same level of experience seem to relate to their general style or approach to planning. In essence, some teachers feel more secure and relaxed about the tasks of teaching if a lesson has been well planned. Others, to some extent, need the pressure generated by the close onset of a lesson to concentrate their minds to the task at hand. Certainly, the ideal approach will be one in which the teacher is able to devote some time, well in advance, to the planning of each lesson. The reality of life as a teacher, however, is that there are many competing demands on your time. The amount of time for planning is thus somewhat constrained. As a result, more extensive and formal planning is likely to focus on those lessons where something new or more demanding will take place.

Flexibility

Another very important aspect of planning is the need to be flexible about the implementation of your plans. Effective teaching depends on the ability to monitor, adapt and develop what goes on in the classroom in the light of how pupils behave during the lesson. No matter how careful and well thought out the planning of the

Be flexible in your lesson planning

lesson was, once it starts, the immediate demands of how things are going, take complete precedence.

It may become apparent that some of the ideas you intended to introduce and discuss at length appear to be well understood by pupils already or are much more difficult to understand than you envisaged; or you may notice that a large number of pupils are having difficulties in carrying out a task you had set and which you had planned to allow them to undertake largely uninterrupted for most of the lesson. In such circumstances, a change in your original plan would be appropriate to ensure that the pupils' needs were being met.

Unfortunately, beginning teachers are occasionally in the position of reaping the worst of both worlds. They invest a great deal of time and energy in preparing their plan for a lesson and at the same time have a greater need to be flexible and adapt their plan in the light of ongoing feedback. Thus, for example, a worksheet may have been carefully prepared only to find the tasks set are too difficult, and a swift change to whole class teaching may be required. For experienced teachers, such a situation is less likely to occur, but if it did, changing to another activity would pose little problem. For the beginning teacher, this situation is more likely, and the difficulty of switching to an unprepared activity is more demanding. Indeed, because of this, student teachers are particularly likely to persist with their original plan unless the problems arising are much more acute and, until they build up experience, are more often than not wise to do so. In contrast, changing horses in mid-stream, to switch from one activity to a more appropriate one, is almost a skill of delight for the experienced teacher, in the extent to which it calls upon their professional knowledge and experience to be able to do so successfully.

Developing lesson planning skills

A major difference between beginning teachers and experienced teachers is the latter's ability to take a longer view of how a whole sequence of lessons will fit together. Indeed, experienced teachers tend to be much more aware of the end point of learning that they want pupils to have reached after dealing with a topic over several weeks, whereas beginning teachers tend to focus much more on the short-term learning outcomes for a particular lesson. This is well illustrated in a detailed case study of a secondary school English teacher reported by McCutcheon and Milner (2002); it shows the way the teacher was able to draw upon his rich content knowledge in planning lessons, and the way he viewed the planning of individual lessons and his thinking about interconnected themes, and which curriculum materials and activities to employ, as being very much subordinate to his overall long-term perspective on planning.

Another major difference is the degree of pedagogical content knowledge (knowledge about how to teach particular topics) that experienced teachers are able to draw upon when planning lessons. Having taught a particular topic several times, experienced teachers are very much aware of the difficulties involved in teaching that topic, and the areas where the pupils' understanding may need to be developed and strengthened. They are also more aware of what aspects of the topic are the key elements that need to be grasped, and how much time needs to be devoted to doing this. It is sometimes claimed that an experienced teacher should be able 'at the drop of a hat' to teach an acceptable lesson on any topic in their area. They would probably first of all want to know something about the pupils' age, general ability and motivation; they would then want information on what the pupils already knew about the topic (this would probably also be checked at the start of the lesson by having a question and answer session). After that, the teacher's experience of having taught this topic before with different groups of pupils would be enough to provide the teacher with a clear idea of how to organise the lesson. Beginning teachers lack this wealth of pedagogical content knowledge. A study by Van Der Valk and Broekman (1999) explored student teachers' pedagogical content knowledge by asking student teachers to prepare a lesson plan about a topic as if they had to teach it, and then interviewed the student teachers about their lesson plans. These interviews provided a very useful way of exploring their pedagogical content knowledge. Indeed, feedback from tutors and mentors on lesson plans provides a very important learning experience for beginning teachers in developing their lesson planning skills.

Lesson planning

As noted earlier, there are four major elements involved in lesson planning:

- deciding on educational objectives
- selecting and scripting a lesson
- preparing the materials and resources to be used
- deciding how to monitor and assess pupils' progress.

The preparation of materials and resources will be considered in the final section of this chapter. The other three elements will be the focus of our attention in this section.

Deciding on educational objectives

The most important aspect of an educational objective is that it is a description of an aspect of pupil learning. To gain knowledge about prime numbers, to understand the nature of causality in History, to acquire the skill of drawing a river's path to the sea through contour lines, or to feel empathy for the victims of the slave trade, would all be examples of educational objectives for a lesson contributing to pupils' intellectual development.

To develop the skills involved in co-operating with other pupils, to become more able to listen attentively to other pupils' statements during class discussion, and to feel more confident about one's own capabilities in the subject, would be examples of educational objectives for a lesson contributing to pupils' social development.

Educational objectives cannot be stated in terms of what pupils will be doing, such as working through an exercise, drawing a map or small group discussion. These are activities used to *promote* learning. The educational objectives must describe what is to *constitute* the learning. One of the major pitfalls in teaching is to neglect thinking precisely about educational objectives and to see planning as simply organising activities. While the two go hand in hand, it is all too easy to think that a lesson that went well logistically was effective (i.e. the pupils did what you intended), until you ask yourself what the pupils actually learned.

In selecting your objectives, a great deal of thought needs to be given to how these objectives relate to previous and future work the pupils are involved in, and how appropriate they are to extending their current abilities, attitudes and interests. For example, in deciding to introduce the notion of prime numbers, do the pupils already have an adequate grasp of what it means for numbers to have factors? Indeed, linking new learning to previous learning is immensely important, and particularly effective if the new learning can be seen to grow out of the previous learning. Thus a lesson on prime numbers may first of all utilise an activity in which pupils can apply their previous knowledge and understanding of factors (this will check that all is well on that front). They may then identify numbers only divisible by one and itself, which are then given a special name (prime numbers). This would combine a linking of previous learning with a sense of discovery and growth, and also extend the previous learning.

Selecting content

Selecting the content for a lesson involves a number of considerations. Even working within the framework of the National Curriculum still leaves a great deal of choice to teachers. The selection of content will clearly need to relate to the overall programme of study for pupils, but the decision on how much emphasis to give to particular topics will depend on the teacher's view of its importance and difficulty.

Indeed, a very important teaching skill is that of separating a topic into distinct elements or aspects, and designing a sequence or progression through these elements that makes coherent and intellectual sense and effectively facilitates learning. One of the most demanding aspects for beginning teachers is trying to decide how best to do this in a way that satisfactorily meets the pupils' needs. This demands good subject knowledge by the teacher, an awareness of how to separate and sequence the elements of the topic, and an awareness of pupils' needs. Beginning teachers tend to rely somewhat on established practice in the school, particularly if a scheme of work is in use (such as that based on a textbook or worksheets). With experience, however, teachers become much more confident and authoritative in deciding on the nature and structure of the content they wish to use, and also better able to judge the pace of progress to expect through the content elements and the likely areas of difficulty or misunderstanding that may arise. The problem for experienced teachers becomes that of keeping abreast of developments in the teaching of their subject and topics in line with changes in required educational attainment.

Selecting learning activities

The selection of learning activities offers much scope and choice for teachers. The decision about which activity or combination of activities to use within a lesson depends on the teacher's beliefs about the relative effectiveness of the different activities for the type of learning intended. This decision, however, also needs to take account of a range of factors relating to the context of the lesson.

First, will the activities selected meet the needs of this particular group of pupils, taking account of their abilities, interests and motivation, and the way they are likely to respond to these activities? You may feel that because a particular class seems to work well when group work tasks are used, you will incorporate group work into their lesson. Equally well, you may decide to incorporate group work into the lesson because the class has not worked well with this activity, and you feel more practice and experience with this activity will be of value to them in developing associated skills and benefits. Indeed, the fact that an activity has not worked well may suggest a need to use it more often rather than to avoid using it.

A second important factor concerns when the lesson occurs. The type of activities that might be effective on a Friday afternoon, or following morning assembly, or extending work done in a previous lesson when a number of learning difficulties were encountered, may be influenced by this context.

Third, such planning decisions are also influenced by logistics, other demands and time pressures facing the teacher. A lesson that requires a lot of planning effort and preparation is perhaps best avoided in the middle of a week in which you have to mark a heavy load of examination scripts, or when you know that the particular equipment needed is in great demand for other activities.

The variety and appropriateness of activities

When thinking about the learning activities to be used, you also need to think of the lesson as a coherent whole, such that the total package of experience provided for pupils achieves your intended learning outcomes. As such, not only must the activities deliver the appropriate intellectual experience for this learning to occur, but also facilitate the ease with which pupils can engage and remain engaged in this experience.

The activities must thus elicit and sustain pupils' attention, interest and motivation. Even when interest and motivation are high, pupils will find it difficult to listen to a teacher's exposition for a long period; doubly so if they are young or the exposition is difficult or unclear, or if it is a hot day. As such, most lessons will involve some variety of activities. The initial phase of the lesson may be designed to set the scene and elicit interest, the major part of the lesson may involve the main learning experiences, and the ending may involve some review or general comments about the importance, relevance or quality of the learning that took place.

While a variety of activities is important, each activity must be appropriate to the learning at hand. Thus, for example, developing pupils' ability to articulate and communicate their ideas orally is much more likely to be achieved through practice, feedback and critiquing others, rather than by extensive reading about how to do it (although this may play a useful part). A variety of activities also provides pupils with an opportunity to learn in different ways, and thereby to build up and develop the skills to do so effectively. At the same time, however, this does not mean that every lesson must involve a variety of activities. It is just as important to provide extended periods of work based on one type of task in order to allow pupils to develop the skills of organising and sustaining their concentration and effort, particularly in relation to a task where the quality of what is produced depends on the marshalling and development of the work undertaken (in contrast to a simply repetitive task).

Using ICT

When using information and communication technology (ICT), you need to take extra care to check the educational purpose for its use. Is it to help develop pupils' ICT skills? Is it to illustrate to pupils how ICT can be used to explore the topic in hand? Is it to motivate the pupils? Is it to encourage pupils to work in a particular way, e.g. individualised work, small group work? Is it to develop a deeper understanding of the topic? All these different purposes are valid, but you need to be sure what you intend for the use of ICT in this particular lesson.

The type of ICT and the way you use it might need to be quite different if you are primarily using it to motivate pupils compared with when you are trying to foster a higher quality of understanding of the topic. Research on the impact of ICT on pupils and their learning indicates that teachers need to develop two sets of skills when using ICT: (i) being able to use the ICT with adequate technical competence; and (ii) being able to use the ICT in a way that promotes higher-quality pupil learning. Teachers need to master the first set of skills before they can develop expertise in the second set of skills (this is also true for pupils). Recognising the purpose you have for using ICT will enable you to check that you have developed the necessary skills which go hand in hand with the particular purpose you have in mind for its use (Leask and Pachler, 2005; Wheeler, 2005).

Of particular importance when planning to use ICT, is being able to move beyond the stage of using ICT simply as a means of engaging pupils in the work (the so-called 'whizz-bang' approach) to being able to use ICT to enhance pupils' deeper understanding of the subject matter. Whilst using ICT can act as a powerful motivator for pupils in the short term (and that's fine as far as it goes), it is only when pupils use ICT in a way that promotes their learning more effectively that a sustained impact on their self-confidence and attainment can be realised. This, of course, places demands on you to develop your ICT skills to support your teaching. This is recognised by the inclusion of ICT skills development for student teachers in the TDA (2007) QTS standards to support their teaching and wider professional activities.

Monitoring and assessing pupils' progress

Once the lesson has begun, you will need to monitor and assess pupils' progress and attainment to ensure that the lesson is being effective and is likely to deliver the pupil learning intended (Clarke, 2005). At the same time, this will also give you feedback on what aspects of the lesson, as originally planned, need ongoing modification and adaptation to maintain effectiveness. This requires more than just being responsive and reactive to feedback, such as waiting for a pupil to say they do not understand how to approach the task set. Rather, it requires you to be active, and to probe, question, check and test whether the progress and attainment intended is occurring.

While there is much feedback available to the teacher simply by looking at pupils' facial expressions or responding to those who confess to having difficulties, all too often most pupils will adopt strategies and techniques which indicate superficially that they understand and can do the work set. Only when exercise books are collected in, or questions asked at the end of the lesson, or subsequent tests are given, might it become evident that much less learning was going on than appeared to be the case.

Unfortunately, it is all too easy to avoid active probing of progress and attainment; if the lesson appears to be going well, you naturally feel that to do so will be making problems for yourself that will need to be dealt with. It requires a great deal of integrity on the teacher's part to, in essence, look for trouble. However, that is in fact the very cutting edge of the skill involved here. Simply approaching a pupil who appears to be

You should regularly assess your pupils' progress

working well and asking the question 'How are things going?' and probing with a few telling questions, can often reveal difficulties that either the pupil was not aware of, or was even deliberately trying to avoid you noticing. It is important to be aware of just how well some pupils manage to avoid being noticed by teachers, by avoiding eye contact and appearing to be working well whenever the teacher is nearby. The 'ripple effect' refers to the way pupils appear to be working hard at the task in hand when the teacher walks around the room, with those pupils the teacher is approaching having their eyes glued to their work, whilst those pupils whom the teacher has just passed start to relax, and in some cases resume talking to their neighbour.

Such active monitoring and assessment of pupils requires some forethought and planning. At what stages during the lesson, and how, are you going to get the necessary feedback? For example, one may usefully use a transition period between one activity and another for some quick whole class questioning and discussion about what was covered and whether any problems have arisen. This does not mean that every lesson must have some in-built testing of attainment; rather, a more subtle form of ongoing probing and reviewing should be employed that will be sufficient to enable the teacher to feel confident that the intended learning is occurring. Nevertheless, there is a role here for formal tests from time to time, and also the use of homework to explicitly probe the learning covered as well as to generate new learning.

Lesson preparation

Preparation primarily refers to the preparation of all the resources and materials to be used in the lesson, including the writing and running off of copies of worksheets, the ordering, delivery and checking of equipment, arranging desks and chairs in the required layout, and making notes about the content of the lesson to be presented Clearly, planning and preparation go hand in hand, and many planning decisions are taken while preparation is going on. Nevertheless, there are a number of important skills involved in preparation that are worthy of attention and may be crucial to the effectiveness of the lesson.

Showing you care

The care and effort that teachers take over preparation can have a major positive impact on pupils' sense that the teacher cares about their learning and that the activities to be undertaken are worthwhile and important. In contrast, a lack of preparation, such as may be evident if the teacher has to leave the room at a crucial point to find some statistical tables that need to be handed out, does not simply disrupt the flow of the lesson, but may be perceived by pupils as insulting to their sense of worth as learners (if our learning was really important, the teacher would have prepared better).

While such problems will arise from time to time even in the best prepared circumstances, and pupils will tolerate these, the regular occurrence of poor preparation must be avoided. To be able to say in the middle of a lesson, 'I have already prepared for you . . .', and then reveal some materials, equipment, or using PowerPoint to display a diagram or set of key questions, can have a marked rousing effect on pupils' self-esteem, enthusiasm and sense of purpose for the next part of the lesson.

Rehearsal, checking and back-up

The use of any sort of equipment always poses potential problems for the teacher. Three key words are relevant here: rehearsal, checking and back-up. If you are going to use equipment or materials for any sort of experiment or practical work, you will often find it useful and worthwhile to have a rehearsal of some sort before you deliver that lesson for the first time. Practicals that appear to be virtually problem-proof can have surprises in store for you. For example, you may find that the length of time it takes for a particular effect to be visible takes much longer than you had planned for; or that connecting to the internet is particularly slow.

Another problem can arise if the equipment available is different in some form from that you have used in the past. Some lessons will also require testing the equipment for its purpose. For example, if you are going to take a group of pupils pond-dipping, you may want to check on the type of creatures currently in the pond and whether the jars, nets or whatever is needed are available. Another aspect of rehearsal involves trying to experience the use of the equipment and materials from the pupils' perspective. In preparing an overhead transparency, for example, is what is projected onto the screen clear and readable from the back of the classroom? In using an audio-tape, is the sound clear at the back of the room? In making a construction from card, is the card too flimsy or too thick for its purpose? Is the visual display of material on a laptop sufficiently clear for the task in hand?

Checking simply refers to the need to ensure, shortly before the lesson is due to start, that the resources needed are to hand and in good working order. For anything electrical, this is almost mandatory. Such checking is made easier if you have marked on your lesson notes those items that need a check in this way. Nevertheless, even with adequate rehearsal and checking, things will happen that require a change in your lesson plan. It is here that some thought to back-up can be extremely helpful. While you cannot have a back-up for every piece of equipment, as a matter of regular practice, it is always worth having, for example, a spare light bulb for an overhead projector. More appropriately, you do need to think of what you will do if a particular piece of equipment fails, or if the lesson grinds to halt for some other reason. In planning a lesson, some thought, even if only limited, can be usefully devoted to how another part of the lesson or some alternative activity can be used to good effect if problems arise.

Teaching materials

Worksheets, overhead transparencies, task cards and ICT software packages are commonly employed in schools, and their design and use involve a number of preparation skills. Often it is important to regard such preparation as a team activity, shared with colleagues, rather than something you do in isolation. Resources of this sort can be used many times over and, as such, if they can be designed to fit well into the programmes of study, are also used by colleagues, and can be linked carefully to assessment tasks, then the time spent in producing high-quality items will be well worthwhile.

However, before embarking on such preparation, it is a good idea to explore whether such resources are already available and can be purchased, borrowed or copied. Some textbook schemes provide a set of parallel worksheets that can be used. Websites often contain a whole host of well-prepared resources of a high quality that can be adapted and used for your purposes. Some schools have gone to great lengths to develop and catalogue materials into a resource centre, either school-wide or subject-specific, and some teachers have similarly indexed materials (including pictures and various artefacts) which they have in their personal possession or have easy access to.

There are many excellent resources and activity packs now published, including mathematical games, facsimile documents for historical analysis, and ICT simulations, all of a quality well beyond that which teachers can normally produce. However, there is a danger in using such materials, particularly ones that have been commercially produced and look very attractive. The danger is that one can be misled into thinking that because such materials have been produced at a high level of quality in appearance, then effective learning is likely to follow from their use. In fact, it is extremely important for the teacher to carefully consider what learning will actually follow from their use, in order to ensure that the educational outcomes intended are realised.

In preparing worksheets, task cards or similar types of materials, quality of presentation is of the highest importance. They need to be well laid out, not contain too much information, and should attempt to elicit pupils' interest. Particular attention needs to be paid to the language used; you need to be sure it is neither too simple nor too difficult for the range of pupil ability for whom it is intended. You also need to give careful thought as to whether such materials are going to be introduced by you and supplemented with various instructions, or whether they are to be self-explanatory. Worksheets and task cards can range from simple exercises and tasks aimed at extracting facts from what is given to answer the questions posed, to quite sophisticated materials aimed to give pupils an opportunity for creative analysis.

An example of the former is a worksheet on percentages containing cut-out adverts from a newspaper concerning the prices of various items with percentage reductions; questions here involve calculating which items are the best buys. An example of the latter is a series of line-drawn pictures (as in children's comics) about which pupils have to write a story. As well as examples designed to be used by individual pupils, other materials can be designed for small group work, such as using a facsimile of a letter written by a king as a source of evidence to interpret a historical event (also taking account of when and to whom the letter was written as part of the discussion of the letter as valid evidence); here the use of small group discussion may highlight the extent to which the interpretation and validity of evidence involve personal judgements.

Assessment materials

Preparation skills also include the need to prepare assessment materials. Indeed, the monitoring of pupils' progress and attainment throughout their school careers requires a formal and regular record to be kept. While some of this will involve formal tests given at the end of periods of study, much assessment is also based on observing performance during normal classroom activity.

This is particularly so in relation to monitoring the development of various pupil skills defined in the National Curriculum. This requires that appropriate assessments are prepared and built into the planning of lessons, and a formal note made of pupils' performance. This means that some activities in the lesson will be deliberately planned with a view to an assessment being made. As such, the activity must offer a fair opportunity to monitor the performance being examined. Two important planning decisions are involved here. First, how many pupils will you attempt to assess in a particular lesson (one, several, all)? Second, what procedures will you adopt? (Will you tell pupils that a formal assessment is being made? Will you help pupils having difficulties during the assessment and, if so, how will you take this into account in your recording?)

In designing assessment materials to be used during normal classroom activity, particular care needs to be taken to ensure that they validly explore the learning you intend to examine. This involves not only assessing what it purports to assess, but assessing it in the way and to the degree required. Consider, for example, the following two framework planning objectives for design and technology, which can be linked to the DfES Key Stage 3 National Strategy for developing thinking skills (DfES, 2005a):

- Pupils should be taught to predict and manage the time needed to complete a short task.
- Pupils should be taught to prepare an ordered sequence for managing the task.

The DfES (2005a) illustrate how these can then be developed into the following two objectives for year 7 pupils in a design and technology lesson:

- Pupils should evaluate group and individual processes used in recreating the instructions for using a construction kit.
- Pupils should analyse how the components of a LEGO construction kit fit together to make a complete model.

Before being able to even begin to prepare for the assessment of these pupils' performance in this lesson, the teacher will need to be clear about what exactly is being assessed and how, and how the assessment will be recorded. In addition, for such assessments to be fair, the assessment materials and procedures adopted will need to be standardised so that each pupil is assessed in the same way. For example, in this lesson, the teacher might prepare a set of levels of success criteria, and then identify the extent to which each pupil's performance matched a particular level of success criteria.

Record keeping

Advanced thought and planning about how records are to be made and kept is also required. These will almost certainly need to be developed and agreed with other colleagues, so that the school's records will be consistent and coherent as the pupils progress through their school careers. A variety of assessment materials need to be used and types of responses given (based on direct observations of pupils' behaviour, questioning in verbal and written form, paper and pencil tests, and derived from normal coursework, including homework). This includes ICT designed to track pupils' progress against national attainment targets and programmes of study.

Preparing yourself and pupils

Another aspect of preparation is the need to prepare yourself. While most teachers can teach most topics most of the time with little need to stimulate their subject knowledge, there will be some topics where you will need to learn about the topic in advance of teaching about it. In that sense, you need to stay one jump ahead of the pupils. Indeed, in areas of rapid curriculum development, you may be hard pressed to do this. This means that private study of particular topics will be needed, ranging from making use of appropriate teacher guides that are available, to attending formal courses or workshop activities for teachers. At its best, the need to do this can add a sense of freshness and curiosity for these topics that you can share and delight in with your pupils.

The TDA (2007) QTS standards include the need for student teachers to have a secure knowledge and understanding of their subjects / curriculum areas and how these relate to the age and ability range they are teaching and to the relevant aspects of the National Strategies.

In addition, you must consider whether pupils need to be prepared in any way. You may need to give them advance warning of certain topics, particularly if they will have to do some preparatory reading, revise some previous work, or bring certain equipment or articles with them. In such circumstances, you also need to check that they are prepared as required, and you may need to have spares of the equipment available. Indeed, in some schools, having spare pens to hand is almost essential for the smooth running of lessons.

Preparing pupils to use ICT, such as interactive whiteboards, laptops and graphic calculators, is particularly important, in order to ensure that pupils do not feel threatened or marginalised by lacking the required ICT skills when using such equipment during the lesson. Indeed, a whole class interactive style of teaching using ICT will generate a lot of pupil frustration if the necessary ICT skills have not been developed and practised first.

Further reading

Butt, G. (2006) *Lesson Planning,* 2nd edn. London: Kogan Page. An excellent, succinct and clear overview of the key issues involved in lesson planning.

Clarke, S. (2005) *Formative Assessment in Action: Weaving the Elements Together.* London: Hodder Murray. Illustrates with practical examples how planning lessons which have clear lesson objectives and success criteria are needed to provide a basis for high-quality formative assessment.

Gronlund, N. E. T. and Nivaldo, J. (2004) *Writing Instructional Objectives for Teaching and Assessment,* 7th edn. Englewood Cliffs: Prentice Hall. A clear and comprehensive analysis of the different types of learning outcomes and how these can form a basis for setting instructional objectives for a lesson.

Tileston, D. W. (2004) *What Every Teacher Should Know About Instructional Planning*. London: Corwin. A clear and readable analysis of the stages involved in planning lessons that takes account of what pupils need to know and be able to do, and how to make learning experiences meaningful.

Key questions about your planning and preparation

1 Are my educational objectives for this lesson clear?
2 Do my educational objectives take appropriate account of pupils' needs, particularly in terms of their abilities, interests, motivation, the context of the lesson and the work they have previously done and will do in the future as part of their programme of study?
3 Does the content matter of the lesson and the learning activities selected, together with the structure of the lesson, appear appropriate to maintain pupils' interest and motivation, and deliver the educational objectives intended?
4 What type of pupil performance during the lessons can I expect, and how do I monitor and explore pupils' progress to ensure that the lesson is effectively promoting the intended pupil learning?
5 Are all the materials, resources and equipment I require well prepared and checked?
6 Does my lesson plan contain all the notes I need to refer to, including, for example, worked examples or a note about extension work to be used if the need arises?
7 Have I adequately prepared pupils for this lesson, by alerting them in advance to any revision that may be required or preparation they should do beforehand?
8 Am I prepared for this lesson, in terms of my subject matter knowledge about the topic to be covered?
9 What type of assessment will I be conducting during the lesson, and, if formal assessment is occurring, is this well-planned and prepared?
10 Are there any particular concerns that I need to bear in mind regarding this lesson, such as a pupil with special educational needs, or a particular aspect of the topic or learning activity that will require careful monitoring?

3 Lesson presentation

Lesson presentation refers to the learning experiences you set up to achieve the intended learning outcomes by pupils. As a result of the many different types of teaching methods that have been developed, there is now a staggering range of learning activities available that can be deployed to good effect. These include, by way of example, exposition, practicals, worksheets, ICT, role play and small group discussion. Moreover, teachers are actively encouraged and expected to make use of a variety of teaching methods in their programme of lessons.

In considering learning activities that a teacher can use, a useful distinction can be made between those activities largely dependent on teacher talk and those that can proceed with little or no direct teacher participation. The former includes teacher exposition, teacher questioning and, to a greater or lesser extent, classroom discussion channelled through the teacher. I shall call the former *teacher talk activities*. The latter includes, for example, practicals, investigation and problem-solving activities, worksheets, ICT, role play and small group discussion. I shall call these *academic tasks*. These two classes of activities will be discussed later in this chapter. Before doing so, however, it is important to consider first of all another aspect of lesson presentation: the teacher's manner.

The teacher's manner

When it comes to lesson presentation, the way that you do it is just as important as what you do. Asking a question with interest conveyed in your tone of voice and facial expression, as opposed to sounding tired and bored, makes a world of difference to the type of response you will get, no matter how appropriate the actual question was. Similarly, circulating around the room to monitor progress and help anyone having difficulties, rather than sitting at your desk at the front marking work from another lesson, also conveys an attitude to pupils about the importance of the lesson. All such cues together create a general impression regarding how much effort you feel it is worthwhile to put into the lesson to ensure pupil learning takes place. To elicit and sustain effective learning by pupils, in general, your manner needs to be confident, relaxed, self-assured and purposeful, and should generate an interest in the lesson. In addition, you need to exude positive expectations concerning the progress you expect to be achieved during the lesson.

Positive cues about your manner

There are a number of skills involved in conveying to pupils that you are confident, relaxed, self-assured and purposeful. However, the most crucial aspect of doing this is that you *are* in fact confident, relaxed, self-assured and purposeful! The starting point is not one of being nervous and anxious, and then thinking how you can convey that you are relaxed and confident. Rather, the starting point should be that by sound planning and preparation, and with developing experience, you will quite naturally and unconsciously convey these positive cues. Nevertheless, there are times, particularly when beginning a career in teaching, or occasionally when things are going wrong, that you will feel anxious. In such circumstances, it is helpful to try to consciously induce a sense of relaxation as far as possible, and also to be aware of the aspects of your behaviour involved in conveying this.

The positive cues are largely conveyed by your facial expression, tone of voice, speech, use of eye contact, gestures and positioning. When you feel nervous, you will naturally tend to look and sound nervous, avoid eye contact, and make awkward or repetitive gestures. As such, when feeling nervous, consciously make an effort to ensure that your speech is fluid, clear and audible, that you maintain regular eye contact with pupils and scan around the classroom, and that you spend time standing centre-stage at the front and erect when appropriate.

For the vast majority of beginning teachers, such skills develop fairly quickly; for others, it takes somewhat longer. Some student teachers appear to feel at home in the classroom from the very first lesson; others only start to feel really relaxed and confident during their first year or two of teaching. It must be recognised, however, that there are some for whom the act of teaching will always be anxiety provoking. For those who are unable to feel at home in the classroom, most will not pursue a career in teaching for long. This largely reflects the fact that although much of the teacher's manner can develop through training and experience, it is in part also bound up with the teacher's personality. This is why it is so important for beginning teachers to capitalise on their strengths and mitigate their shortcomings, rather than attempt to model themselves on any particular style of teaching they have witnessed or that is being advocated to them.

Other important aspects of your manner

Over the years there has been much discussion and research on other aspects of the teacher's manner which contribute to effective teaching, and it must be said that no clear and consistent picture has emerged (Borich, 2007; Kyriacou, 1997). Undoubtedly this is because it is possible to be effective through different means. For one teacher, the key to success may largely stem from being firm; for another teacher, it may stem from a warm and caring attitude. Nevertheless, in general it does appear that the quality of conveying enthusiasm and interest for the subject matter at hand is important. Less consistently supported by research evidence, although widely advocated, are the qualities of patience and a sense of humour.

Teacher talk activities

Teachers spend a great deal of their time talking, whether it be lecturing, explaining, giving instructions, asking questions, or directing whole class discussion. As such, it is not surprising that the quality of teacher talk is one of the most important aspects of effective teaching. Indeed, many would claim that it is the most important quality of effective teaching. Communicating effectively with pupils and, in particular, the teacher's effective use of language when using explanations, questions, discussions and plenaries, feature as an important element of the TDA (2007) QTS standards.

Exposition

There is a wealth of research evidence to support the claim that clarity of explanation (often referred to as 'teacher clarity') makes a major contribution to greater educational attainment. Teacher clarity certainly enhances teacher talk activities, and also makes a contribution to the effectiveness of a variety of academic tasks, for example in briefing and debriefing role-play activities, or in the content and layout of a worksheet.

Periods of teacher exposition (i.e. informing, describing and explaining) typically occur throughout a lesson. In schools, it rarely takes the form of a lecture for any great length of time, nor should it, as pupils will find it difficult to pay attention to a lecture, except for a short length of time. Indeed, for this reason, many teachers use a series of questions and the development of pupils' replies to trace out what they want to say, rather than an uninterrupted exposition. This not only involves the pupils more, but also enables you to check on pupils' understanding.

Starting the lesson

What you say at the start of the lesson can be particularly important as it serves a number of functions. First, it must elicit and sustain pupils' attention and interest in the lesson. Establishing a positive attitude at the start of the lesson provides a good springboard for what follows. To create a positive mental set amongst pupils, it is important to ensure that pupils are paying attention when the lesson begins.

Second, it is useful to indicate what the purpose or topic for the lesson is, and its importance or relevance. You will also need to outline the main structure for the lesson (e.g. will there be a starter session or a plenary at the end?). A short warm-up or starter activity can usefully function as a quick recap of a previous lesson or be linked to the topic for the current lesson. In introducing the main part of the lesson, a question to the class, rather than a statement, can usefully arouse their curiosity and induce a problem-solving thrust towards what follows. A fairly quiet but audible voice level is best as it encourages listening, discourages background noise, and makes varying the tone and volume of your delivery easier.

Having elicited attention and indicated the purpose of the lesson, the third function of your introduction may usefully be to alert pupils to any links with previous lessons they need to be aware of, or any particular problems or aspects of this lesson they should be alert to, in order to best prepare them for what is to follow. Such preparation may include practical matters concerning the equipment they will need to use or the pace at which they will be expected to work.

Finally, you can discuss and share with pupils how the main learning intentions will be linked to success criteria and targets for learning, and whether the lesson will be linked to subsequent lessons and to a homework activity.

Effective explaining

Explaining often goes hand in hand with questioning, with the teacher switching from one to the other as and when appropriate. Often this switch is influenced by whether the teacher feels it is appropriate to pull ideas together swiftly to facilitate a move to the next phase of the lesson, using a synthesising statement, or whether the teacher feels more involvement and probing of pupils' ideas is needed. For both explaining and questioning, it is particularly important to ensure that the nature and complexity of the language used by the teacher is at an appropriate level for pupils to understand. Indeed, the skill of the teacher to pitch language use appropriately by taking account of pupils' current level of understanding is one of the most important skills the beginning teacher needs to master.

Writings and research on explaining (Kerry, 2002; Wragg and Brown, 2001a,b) have highlighted seven key aspects involved in enhancing the effectiveness of an explanation:

- *Clarity:* it is clear and pitched at the appropriate level.
- *Structure:* the major ideas are broken down into meaningful segments and linked together in a logical order.
- *Length:* it is fairly brief and may be interspersed with questions and other activities.
- *Attention:* the delivery makes good use of voice and body language to sustain attention and interest.
- *Language:* it avoids use of over-complex language and explains new terms.
- *Exemplars:* it uses examples, particularly ones relating to pupils' experiences and interests.
- *Understanding:* the teacher monitors and checks pupils' understanding.

Perhaps the most important aspect of explaining, however, is the skill in deciding the size of step that pupils can take in going from what they know at the start of the lesson to the learning you intend will take place by the end of the lesson. This decision about the size of step has crucial implications for the type and sophistication of the explanations offered.

In summary, explanations should, by and large, be grammatically simple, make good use of examples, define any technical terms and, most importantly, not go on for too long!

Questioning

Questioning skills are also central to the repertoire of effective teaching (Kerry, 2002; Walsh and Settes, 2005; Wragg and Brown, 2001c,d). There can be few professions to compare with teaching where you spend so much time every day asking questions to which you already know the answer. Research studies looking at teachers' use of questioning has identified the various reasons given by teachers for asking questions as follows:

- to encourage thought, understanding of ideas, phenomena, procedures and values
- to check understanding, knowledge and skills
- to gain attention to task, enable teacher to move towards teaching points, as a 'warm-up' activity for pupils
- to review, revise, recall, reinforce recently learned points, remind about earlier procedures

- for management, settling down, to stop calling out by pupils, to direct attention to teacher or text, to warn of precautions
- specifically to teach whole class through pupil answers
- to give everyone a chance to answer
- to prompt bright pupils to encourage others
- to draw in shyer pupils
- to probe pupils' knowledge after critical answers, re-direct questions to pupil who asked or to other pupils
- to allow expressions of feelings, views and empathy.

Types of questions

A useful distinction can be made between 'open' and 'closed' questions. Open questions can have a number of right answers, whereas closed questions will only have one right answer. Another useful distinction can be made between 'higher order' questions and 'lower order' questions. Higher order questions involve reasoning, analysis and evaluation, whereas lower order questions are concerned with simple recall or comprehension.

Much research indicates that teachers overwhelmingly ask more closed and lower order questions than open and higher order questions. While, in general, open and higher order questions are more intellectually demanding and stimulating, and research does indicate that more of these types should be used, one does need to bear in mind the range of purposes behind asking questions, as indicated earlier. Given that open and higher order questions are more time consuming, it would be difficult to use these very frequently without constraining other intentions, such as the need to maintain an appropriate pace to the lesson, or to involve most of the pupils. As with all aspects of teaching skills, a balance is required in meeting a range of different intentions at the same time.

Effective questioning

Kerry (2002) has highlighted seven questioning skills:

- pitching the language and content level of questions appropriately for the class
- distributing questions around the class
- prompting and giving clues when necessary
- using pupils' responses (even incorrect ones) in a positive way
- timing questions and pauses between questions
- learning to make progressively greater cognitive demands through sequences of higher order questions
- using written questions effectively.

When asking questions there are two extremely important points to bear in mind. First, answering a question, particularly in front of classmates, is an emotionally high-risk activity. As such, it is essential that the classroom climate during questioning is one of support and respect for the pupil's answer (both by the teacher and by other pupils). Second, do not allow some pupils to opt out of questioning. It is evident that some pupils are adept at avoiding being noticed and will do whatever they can to terminate quickly any interaction with the teacher. Such pupils need to be involved and helped to contribute to the lesson.

A number of features characterise skilful questioning. It is a useful technique not to name the pupil whom you want to answer the question until you have finished the question. This helps to ensure that all pupils are attentive. When asking the question, try to ensure that it is as clear and unambiguous as possible. If the pupil is in difficulties, it can be useful to rephrase the question in a different way or guide the pupil towards an answer through the use of scaffolding (see later in this chapter for a description of scaffolding). Allowing pupils some time to talk to partners and to share answers can be useful in promoting higher-quality thinking.

Most importantly, ask the question in a manner that conveys you are interested in the reply, maintain eye contact with the pupil and ensure that other pupils have the courtesy to listen in silence. When prompting or helping a pupil, remember that the object of this is to assist the pupil's thinking, not to enable the correct answer to be guessed from the clues given. Finally, it is often worthwhile to check how a pupil arrived at the answer given (whether right or wrong), as this can give you some useful insight into the thinking involved.

Directing classroom discussion

Directing classroom discussion

The third area of teacher talk activities to be considered here is that of classroom discussion channelled through the teacher: a mixture of teacher and pupil explanations, views and questions. Classroom discussion begins at the point when pupils ask questions and when one pupil responds to what another pupil has said.

When classroom discussion takes place, there are two key decisions you need to take. First, you need to consider how best to lay the room out (is it appropriate to organise pupils so that they can see and hear each other?). Second, you need to consider the extent to which you are going to direct the discussion and make a leading contribution to shaping the flow and development of what is said.

In using classroom discussion to good effect, it is useful to indicate the purpose of having such a discussion, to indicate how long the discussion is intended to last, and to summarise at the end what conclusions can be drawn. It is particularly important to remember that one of the prime reasons for having classroom discussion is to give pupils the opportunity to develop and express their ideas. This will need encouragement, and a tolerance to allow badly formed and incorrect notions to be expressed (ensuring that any errors become apparent as the discussion develops, rather than interrupted or shot down immediately).

Whole-class interactive teaching

In recent years a style of teaching referred to as whole-class interactive teaching has been widely advocated (Moyles *et al.,* 2003; Hayes, D. 2006). This style of teaching involves the skilful use of exposition and questioning to engage pupils in higher level thinking about the topic in hand. This is often characterised as being done with pace, in order to sustain a lively and buoyant feel to the lesson, but the teacher also needs to give pupils adequate thinking time when appropriate in order to allow higher-quality responses to questions. A teacher will typically also give pupils short tasks to do or ask them to talk in pairs for a few minutes before asking for answers. Unfortunately, in unskilled hands, this style of teaching can regress back into a more conventional whole-class (exposition-based) teaching. Indeed, a study by Smith *et al.* (2004) looking at the quality of interactive whole class teaching in the National Literacy and Numeracy Strategies reported that traditional patterns of whole class interaction have not been dramatically transformed by the Strategies. The skills needed lie in being able to sustain pupils' engagement and contributions, and in particular to ensure that less able pupils and more socially reserved pupils in the class do not feel intimidated by this style of teaching. At its best, pupils will be encouraged to argue with and comment on both what the teacher says and on what other pupils have said. Generating high-quality pupil talk in this way is perhaps one of the most challenging and important tasks facing being teachers (Myhill *et al.,* 2006).

Academic tasks

Academic tasks refer to activities set up by teachers to facilitate pupil learning, which can proceed with little or no direct teacher participation once they are up and running.

Examples include doing experiments or other practical tasks, investigation and problem-solving activities, worksheets, ICT, role play and small group discussion. Almost all such activities tend to involve the teacher circulating around and monitoring progress, giving individual help as and when necessary. Nevertheless, some teachers prefer to maintain a high level of direction during such activities, while others see important educational benefits deriving from being less directive (this point will be developed further when we consider the notion of 'active learning' later in this chapter).

Setting up academic tasks

For academic tasks to be successfully employed, it is absolutely crucial that it is clear to pupils what they have to do, and to indicate the relationship between the task and the learning intended. It is easy to fall into the trap of thinking that the most important aspect is to get the pupils under way quickly with the task and then to deal with any problems as they arise. Doing so can lead to your having to dash from one desk to another throughout the lesson, or else having to interrupt the class as a whole on several occasions. In fact, the most important aspect for success is the careful preparation of the tasks and materials to be used (so that they are clear and, if necessary, self-explanatory) coupled with a clear briefing of what is required before the task is started. Some pupils may not pay attention during this briefing session if they know that you will simply give an individual briefing to anyone who wants one once the work has begun. If several pupils have this attitude, there will be many demands made on you at the start. As such, it is well worthwhile to ensure that as many pupils as possible are clear about the task in hand before the class is allowed to start the work.

Another aspect of academic tasks that is of great importance is to ensure that pupils possess the skills required to undertake the task successfully, or, if not, that the skills are helped to develop. All tasks, whether it be extracting information from a set text, using a worksheet, extracting data from the internet, loading a CD, carrying out an experiment, or participating in small group discussion, involve a number of skills. It is all too easy to assume that pupils already have appropriate skills or can develop these by trial and error. In fact, many pupils get into difficulties simply because they are unsure about how to proceed and what is expected of them.

A nice example of this is that of a teacher asking pupils to spend a lesson writing a poem about winter. Now, for some pupils the processes involved in writing a poem are rather mysterious, and little headway may be made. However, if the teacher was first to spend a lesson composing a poem from scratch on the blackboard in front of the pupils, and demonstrate, by thinking aloud, how one can start from some ideas or phrases and rework these and change words, the whole process for pupils could then be demystified. This demystification is essential for almost all academic tasks. How do you extract information from a set text? How do you make successful use of small group discussion? What steps are involved in conducting an investigation? Paying explicit attention to pupils' learning skills before, during and after academic tasks can have a major impact on the quality of learning which takes place.

One of the advantages of setting work for individuals is that it allows pupils to work at their own pace, it helps them to organise and take responsibility for their own effort, and it enables the work to be structured and tailored to their own level of difficulty (including the provision of extension and enrichment materials and tasks for the more able pupils in the class). Where pupils are working individually on an extended piece of work or a project, or through a work scheme, careful and regular monitoring of progress is essential.

Co-operative activities

Co-operative activities, such as small group discussion or collaborative problem-solving, enable pupils to share ideas, to develop the skills involved in co-operative interaction, to communicate clearly and to work as a team. Generally speaking, a group size ranging from two to six seems to be best for most co-operative tasks. Pairs are most commonly used, in part for logistical reasons and in part because both partners will get more contribution time than when in a larger group. However, it is important to make use of larger groups, which will enable pupils to develop wider communication and organisational skills.

Some teachers, however, are reluctant to make use of co-operative tasks because they fear that by relinquishing tight control over the learning activities, it will be harder to sustain good order. There is little doubt that such activities do depend on good teaching skills, but fortunately with the increasing use of such activities, pupils are more familiar and more skilled at using such activities to good effect than when such activities were relatively novel in schools.

It is important to note that pupils require help and support to use small group co-operative activities effectively. Research indicates that the way the activity is structured can have a positive impact on the quality of learning that takes place. A study by Gillies (2004) identified three key elements of a structured activity:

- The pupils understand what they are expected to do and how they are expected to work together.
- The task is established so that all group members realise they are required to contribute to completing it and to assist others to do likewise.
- Pupils are taught the interpersonal and small group skills needed to promote a sharing and respectful attitude towards others.

Gillies found that pupils in structured groups (as described above) worked together much better and more effectively than pupils working together in unstructured groups.

Active learning

Active learning refers to any activities where pupils are given a marked degree of autonomy and control over the organisation, conduct and direction of the learning activity. Most usually, such activities involve problem-solving and investigational work, and may be individualised (such as an extended piece of work or project) or involve small group collaboration (such as small group discussion, games, a role-play simulation or collaborative project).

In essence, active learning may usefully be contrasted with expository teaching, in which pupils are largely passive receivers of information which is tightly under the teacher's control. A number of educational benefits have been claimed for active learning activities:

- They are intellectually more stimulating and thereby more effective in eliciting and sustaining pupil motivation and interest.
- They are effective in fostering a number of important learning skills involved in the process of organising the activities, such as when organising their own work during individualised activities, and interaction and communication skills during co-operative activities.
- They are likely to be enjoyed, offer opportunity for progress, are less threatening than teacher talk activities and thereby foster pupil attitudes towards themselves as learners and more positive attitudes towards the subject.
- Co-operative activities in particular enable greater insights into the conduct of the learning activities through observing the performance of peers and sharing and discussing procedures and strategies.

In considering active learning, however, you need to be aware that this term has not been used by teachers with any consistency. As well as referring to teaching methods or learning activities, it is sometimes used to refer to the mental experience of learning by discovery. Nevertheless, in the sense of activities such as small group work, teachers are generally expected to make use of such activities as well as teacher talk activities. The message, in effect, is that how pupils learn is as important as the content of what they learn.

In addition, active learning can sometimes offer a much more powerful experience or insight into what is to be learned than expository teaching. For example, in a mathematics lesson a teacher could ask pupils to guess how many pupils fit into a one cubic metre box, and then bring one in and see. Pupils having this experience are thereafter left with a very strong image of what this unit of volume means.

Academic tasks versus teacher talk activities

Much discussion has taken place over the years concerning the relative merits of teachers using whole-class teaching methods based on teacher talk activities compared with the use of academic tasks, particularly those characterised by active learning. Comparisons of educational attainment in different countries coupled with a whole host of research studies of effective teaching suggest that an approach described as 'direct teaching' is probably the most effective approach to promoting higher levels of pupil attainment. Direct teaching essentially consists of lessons that follow five main stages:

- The teacher sets clear goals for the lesson.
- The teacher teaches through exposition of what is to be learned.
- The teacher asks questions to check pupil understanding.
- There is a period of supervised practice.
- The teacher assesses pupils' work to check that the goals have been achieved.

Nevertheless, one should not use such findings to call for teaching to become predominantly based on whole-class teaching methods employing teacher talk activities. It is widely accepted that teachers need to make use of a variety of teaching methods. Doing so helps pupils to develop the skills of learning in different ways and also provides for a greater variety of learning outcomes. What is needed is the right mix of activities.

Teaching styles and learning styles

Discussion of the skills involved in lesson presentation has sometimes made reference to the way in which some teachers seem to adopt a typical approach to their teaching, and also the way in which some pupils seem to have strong preferences about how they prefer to learn. This has given rise to consideration of whether certain teaching approaches may be particularly effective, and whether an attempt should be made by teachers to take account of differences between pupils in their preferences for certain learning activities.

Teaching styles

Studies of classroom practice have attempted to categorise teachers in terms of their *teaching styles,* which refers to their tendency to make frequent use of certain types of learning activities in their teaching (Cohen *et al.,* 2004; McCormick and Leask, 2005). For example, some teachers tend to make much greater use of teacher-centred, exposition-dominated activities, together with teacher-directed seatwork tasks. At its most traditional, this approach may be coupled with the organisation of desks into rows and a great deal of guided practice. This approach has often been described as a 'formal teaching style'. In contrast, some teachers make much greater use of student-centred activities, involving small group work and giving pupils' more control over the direction of their work. This may be coupled with arranging desks together to form groups of pupils seated together, and the use of more open-ended tasks negotiated with pupils. This approach has often been described as an 'informal teaching style'.

Attempts to identify and describe teaching styles, however, have been problematic, because there are a wider variety of styles than can be described (a simple dichotomy between formal and informal, for example, is too simplistic) and most teachers use a mix of styles and also vary their mix of styles from lesson to lesson and from class to class. Nevertheless, some consistent differences between teachers in terms of their general approach to teaching do seem to be discernible.

Learning styles

Similarly, attempts have also been made to describe pupils in terms of their *learning styles* (Pritchard, 2005; Smith, 2005). This term refers to the types of learning activities and tasks pupils prefer to experience and which they feel are more effective in promoting their own learning. It also includes their preferences about the types of strategies for learning they prefer to adopt when given a choice, and their preferences regarding the physical and social characteristics of the learning situation. For example, some pupils prefer to read (rather than listen), work alone (rather than in a group), find things out for themselves (rather than be given a digest by the teacher), and have tasks tightly prescribed (rather than left to their own decision-making).

The point is sometimes made that if pupils are taught more often in their preferred learning style, more learning will take place. As such, teachers should try to match learning activities to pupils' preferences. Whilst I agree that it is important for teachers to be aware that pupils differ in their learning styles, I think the idea of matching of work to pupils' preferred learning styles involves a number of problems. First of all, it is important to help pupils to develop the skills to learn effectively in their non-preferred learning styles, as pupils who are taught overwhelmingly in their preferred learning style may not be able to develop a full range of learning skills. Second, pupils' learning styles are not easy to determine and also vary from lesson to lesson and from subject to subject. Third, the logistics of classroom life would make it extremely difficult to cater differentially for the variety of pupils' learning preferences in the same class.

Personalised learning

The debate about the relative effectiveness of different teaching methods and learning activities is a complex one, and what works best will vary from situation to situation, depending on the type of class taught and the particular type of learning outcomes being fostered. However, one important implication of research on teaching styles and learning styles is that teachers do need to make use of a variety of learning activities in their teaching. In addition, teachers can use their awareness of the differences between pupils in their learning preferences to help sustain each pupil's motivation by making use of their preferred activities when appropriate, and also by providing additional support and encouragement when making use of their non-preferred activities.

The consideration of how teachers can best meet the learning needs of pupils by taking careful account of each pupil's circumstances, ability and motivation, and preferred learning styles, has given rise to the notion of 'personalised learning', which refers to how a school can tailor the curriculum and teaching methods to the specific learning needs of each pupil, and offer each pupil the type of personalised support that will enable them to develop the skills needed to access learning activities to better effect.

The genesis of personalised learning was initially seen as a way of combating disaffection amongst lower-attaining pupils, but it gradually began to be conceived in terms of being good practice to better meet the needs all pupils. Personalised learning has featured heavily in a range of DfES policy statements which have been produced in its drive to improve the quality of education and to raise the levels of pupil attainments (e.g. DfES, 2004c, 2005b).

The DfES also notes that personalised learning needs to be based on the regular assessment of pupil progress to identify each pupil's learning needs in order to teach them accordingly ('assessment for learning'). The essence of personalised learning is for the pupil to experience learning as something that is relevant to their needs and which they can readily engage in with success. Some attempts have also been made to indicate how the development of personalised learning in schools can be informed by research evidence (Pollard and James, 2004).

The importance of personalised learning is reflected in its inclusion as an element of the TDA (2007) QTS standards. Student teachers need to have knowledge and understanding of a range of teaching, learning and behaviour management strategies and to know how to use and adapt them, including how to personalise learning and provide opportunities for all pupils to achieve their potential.

In recent years a number of research reports have highlighted the ways in which the skilful use of ICT can support personalised learning. A number of these reports can be found at the British Educational Communications and Technology Agency (Becta) website (www.becta.org.uk). Becta (2005) argue that ICT can personalise learning by:

- personalising content sources and resources
- providing pathways through content that are personalised to individual pupils' needs
- presenting a range of interfaces appropriate to an individual pupil's level and ability
- facilitating effective assessment and reporting tools
- providing flexibility regarding when, where and with whom pupils learn.

Matching work to pupil ability and needs

Matching the learning experience to the ability level and needs of each pupil in the class is one of the most skilful aspects of teaching. The difficulty of doing this successfully is in part a reflection of the complexity of the teacher's task: namely, that the class may well have about 30 pupils in it, comprising a wide range of ability and needs.

One of the problems facing teachers is that there is a tendency to pitch the lesson towards meeting the needs of the broad middle range of ability within the class, and then to provide additional material, demands or help for those at the extremes. Part of the problem with this approach is that the more able pupils need more enriching and more stimulating demands, not simply more of the same or more difficult work. Similarly, less able pupils also need more enriching and stimulating demands, not simply less of the same or easier work. A number of work schemes based on individualised programmes of work have been particularly successful in enabling this match to occur across a broad range of ability.

The notion of matching work to pupils does not mean setting work at a level that pupils can already do fairly successfully. Rather, it deals with the idea of what pupils of a certain level of ability are able to achieve in the way of new learning. 'Matching the work' thus refers to deciding how much progress pupils can make in a given lesson or over a course of lessons and then pitching the work to achieve the optimal progress the pupils appear to be capable of.

Studies looking at the school factors influencing pupil progress have indicated that a key factor contributing to greater progress was intellectually challenging teaching (McNeil and Sammons, 2006). However, many studies have noted that the match of task demands to pupils indicated that a majority of tasks were not well matched to pupils, in the sense of promoting the optimal progress pupils were capable of. In some cases the tasks were too easy, whilst in other cases they were too difficult.

Setting and streaming

Another approach used to help match work to pupils is that of grouping pupils into narrower ability bands. This can be done by streaming, where pupils in a particular ability band stay together as a group for all lessons and topics; or setting, where pupils are put into a separate ability group for each subject or topic. Reviews of research on the advantages and disadvantages of grouping pupils by ability (Ireson and Hallam, 2002) indicate that such grouping can be very help in terms of:

- allowing pupils to make progress in line with their ability
- making it easier for the teacher to set work that meets the needs of the whole group
- more able pupils not being held back by the less able
- less able pupils not being discouraged by the more able.

At the same time, research has indicated that there are dangers here, most particularly that pupils grouped together into a low-ability band or set may get caught up in a vicious circle of lowered teacher and pupil expectations concerning what they are capable of.

Mixed-ability groups and differentiation

In some schools mixed-ability groups are used. This may be because the small size of the age group or the small number of pupils doing a particular subject or topic does not allow setting. Additionally, some schools wish to make use of the advantages of having mixed-ability groups in allowing pupils from different backgrounds to mix socially and academically, and to avoid having to teach low sets. It is also important to note that all classes of pupils, even those where some selection by attainment has been made, will involve a range of ability.

Differentiation involves adapting the way the work is set and assessed in order to meet the needs of a range of abilities within the same class. Seven types of differentiation have been highlighted:

- *differentiation by task,* where pupils cover the same content but at different levels
- *differentiation by outcome,* where the same general task is set, but it is flexible enough for pupils to work at their own level
- *differentiation by learning activity,* where pupils are required to address the same task at the same level, but in a different way
- *differentiation by pace,* where pupils can cover the same content at the same level but at a different rate
- *differentiation by dialogue,* where the teacher discusses the work with individual pupils in order to tailor the work to their needs
- *differentiation by support,* where the degree of support is tailored to the needs of individual pupils, with less support offering more challenge and opportunity for initiative
- *differentiation by resource,* where the type of resource used (worksheets, internet, graphical calculator) is tailored to the pupil's ability and skills.

These seven types of differentiation are not mutually exclusive, but rather a matter of emphasis.

Inclusion

Inclusion refers to the way in which teaching and learning in a school is organised in a way that enables the school to cater for pupils with a broad range of ability and needs. Some pupils with moderate or severe special educational needs, including those whose behaviour can be regarded as challenging to deal with, are now being taught in mainstream schools when in the past they would have had their special educational needs catered for in special schools. Teachers need to be skilled at handling a wide range of pupils' needs in the classroom, and this may often involve being able to plan and teach with the help of a support teacher (Lewis and Norwich, 2005). The importance of the skills involved in doing this are recognised in the TDA (2007) QTS standards in which student teachers need to:

- know and understand the role of colleagues with specific responsibility for pupils with special educational needs and disabilities and other individual learning needs
- know how to make effective personalised provision for those they teach, including those for whom English is an additional language or who have special educational needs or disabilities, and how to take practical account of diversity and promote equality and inclusion in their teaching.

Skilful matching

One of the useful ways in which teachers can help ensure that a match is achieved is through careful monitoring of pupils' progress and questioning to check understanding. Unfortunately, many pupils are reluctant to confess to difficulties and are likely instead either to do little work in silence, or else to use various strategies to get the work demanded done with little or even incorrect understanding. As such it is of crucial importance that you take the initiative in monitoring progress, rather than wait for difficulties to be drawn to your attention.

Expectations also play a role in sometimes obscuring what pupils are capable of. Most pupils will do slightly less than is typically demanded of them. This can easily result in a downward spiral of teacher demands, if what the teacher demands of each lesson is the level of work that was produced in previous lessons. Hence you need to be consistently conveying expectations of a higher quality of work and progress in each lesson than is typically achieved. This will create an impression of encouraging and expecting a standard just higher than the norm previously produced, but not so much higher that pupils feel discouraged or that you are dissatisfied with genuine effort on their part.

Matching work to pupils also involves the need to take account of pupils' interests and needs. This includes taking advantage of examples and topics and their applications that are likely to be of interest or relevance to the pupils in your class. In addition, as noted earlier in this chapter, it includes providing a variety of ways of working, using both teacher talk activities and a range of academic tasks, so that pupils can build up the skills involved in working successfully in these different ways.

Some pupils will also have particular needs that must be met. These may range from a pupil who is rather shy and needs encouragement to participate, to a pupil who has difficulty producing legible handwriting. Some pupils will require individual attention for their needs to be met. Some pupils may well have a marked learning difficulty and be identified as having a special educational need. In such cases, the teacher may be able to meet these needs, or there may be additional help or resources available. Indeed, all teachers need to be alert to the possibility that a pupil may have a special educational need and to ensure that such needs are identified and met. Learning difficulties may stem from a physical handicap of some sort, a long period of absence from school, very low general ability, or social and emotional problems.

Tutoring

Another aspect of matching work to pupils is the use of one-to-one teaching, sometimes referred to as tutoring. As well as whole-class teaching and the monitoring of progress on academic tasks, teachers also spend much of their time helping individual pupils on a one-to-one basis. This type of help is a crucial part of effective teaching, not only because of the academic support offered, but also because it is a personal and private encounter between you and the pupil. As such, it offers an important opportunity to emphasise your care, support and encouragement for the pupil's progress. It also provides an important opportunity to assess the pupil's general ability and motivation, and to identify any particular needs.

One of the most important aspects involved in skilful tutoring is that of *scaffolding*. The notion of scaffolding deals with how skilful tutoring can involve helping the pupil with a task by directing their attention to the key elements necessary for applying and

A wide variety of resources are available

developing their current understanding, and thereby enabling them to carry out the task successfully. A number of studies of classroom practice have shown that the teacher's ability to do this effectively requires a sensitive awareness of both the pupil's current level of understanding and the subject matter in hand.

The effectiveness of tutoring has long been recognised, and some schools now make use of parents as helpers in the classroom or use other pupils, either the same age or older pupils, to provide additional opportunities for one-to-one help in the classroom. The use of pupils as tutors, often referred to as 'peer tutoring', is fairly widespread and a number of studies have indicated that where pupils are asked to help other pupils in this way (usually with reading or number work), both pupils seem to benefit. Of particular importance in using other adults or pupils as tutors in this way, is that they are carefully briefed about their role and the need to offer encouragement to pupils during the interactions.

Using resources and materials

There is a vast range of resources and materials available for use in the class-room, including interactive whiteboards, laptops, PowerPoint, overhead projector transparencies, CDs, worksheets and simulation materials. Perhaps the golden rule concerning their use is always to check their quality and appropriateness for the lesson. It is all too easy to think that because such resources are going to be used, that is an excuse for accepting a somewhat lower quality or something not quite appropriate for the intended learning. As a result, pupils all too often have to watch videos with poor sound quality or work through a software package that is unclear or even inappropriate to the topic being investigated. While the desire for pupils to acquire a familiarity with such materials may be important enough to warrant this on the odd occasion, you must be rigorous in your appraisal of the suitability of such materials for the learning outcomes you intend.

It is also important to familiarise yourself with the content of such materials if you have not used them before or for some time, since it could prove difficult to deal with any problems that may arise unexpectedly. In addition, since many resources may be used by pupils with little or no help from the teacher, difficulties could arise which you may not be aware of until after the lesson or not at all, unless you carefully monitor progress.

Using the board and projector

The board is still the most widely used teaching aid and the quality of your board use will be a major indicator of your teaching. Well-prepared and clear use of the board is not only effective as a teaching aid, but is also an example to the class of the standard or quality of work and presentation you expect. The board can also usefully be a reminder or record of important points: for example, the spelling of new or difficult words, a note of the task pupils are to undertake when the present task has been completed, or a list of pupils' ideas to be used for later analysis. One pitfall for beginning teachers to note is talking while facing the board. When you are writing on the board and have something important to say, you must turn your head to face the class as you speak.

Similar points can be made about the use of interactive whiteboards and data projectors, although here it is possible to produce materials in advance to good effect. Always ensure that the projection onto the screen is clearly visible from all parts of the classroom, and that you are not obscuring the view yourself (an occasional fault, even amongst some experienced teachers!).

Individualised schemes of work

One marked area of development in the use of resources and materials has been the widespread use of individualised schemes of work based on software packages. One of the skills involved in their effective use concerns the organisation of how and when pupils use these, and how and when they receive feedback on their progress.

Many studies have indicated that one of the key factors in promoting greater pupil attainment is the ability of the teacher to maximise the time that pupils spend educationally benefiting from the learning activity in hand. The more time they spend waiting to use resources or waiting for help when they are in difficulties, the less time they are making progress in their attainment. The procedures used by teachers to ensure good organisation in using such resources is thus of great importance.

One advantage of some software packages is that they are designed to be self-explanatory and often provide feedback about correct answers and help for pupils in difficulties. Nevertheless, most such resources do still require teacher assistance from time to time, and for teachers to be involved in assessing progress. As such, you need to ensure that the arrangements you make allow such time to be given. One particularly useful strategy, more commonly employed in primary schools, is to organise a lesson such that different groups are working on different tasks, ranging from tasks involving minimal teacher contact, to those involving a great deal of contact. By dividing the class up in this way, you will be able to spend more time with those pupils needing your help without this being to the detriment of other pupils.

Another useful strategy is to establish routines or procedures that pupils are required to follow, so that they do not waste time wondering what to do next in a particular situation. A simple rule stating what pupils are expected to do if they get into difficulties or have finished a piece of work, can help to ensure smooth running of classroom activities, and enables you to check whether the activities set are causing problems, are too easy, too difficult, or are unclear in any respect.

Treating resources and materials with care

Finally, when pupils use resources and materials that are to be used again by others, it is worth emphasising that the resources must be handled with care and respect. This is important not only because loss or damage may be costly and also inconvenience other pupils, but also because it highlights that in life everyone will be sharing resources and that such common ownership and use imposes responsibilities and obligations on each user. What is true in this respect within the community of the school is also true for society in general.

Further reading

Borich, G. D. (2007) *Effective Teaching Methods: Research Based Practice,* 6th edn. Englewood Cliffs: Prentice Hall. An excellent overview of our current state of understanding about effective lesson presentation.

Hayes, D. (2006) *The Art of Interactive Teaching.* Exeter: Learning Matters. A readable treatment of the key features involved in interactive teaching.

Kerry, T. (2002) *Explaining and Questioning.* Cheltenham: Nelson Thornes. This book provides an excellent overview of the two teaching skills that are still the stock and trade of an effective teacher's repertoire.

Myhill, D., Jones, S. and Hopper, R. (2006) *Talking, Listening, Learning: Effective Talk in the Primary Classroom.* Maidenhead: Open University Press. An excellent analysis of the way the quality of language used in the classroom affects learning, and the teaching skills involved in sustaining quality talk.

Key questions about your lesson presentation

1 Are the learning activities appropriate to the type of learning outcomes I intend?
2 Do the learning activities take adequate account of pupils' abilities, interests and needs, and of their previous and future learning?
3 Do I make use of a variety of different types of learning activities?
4 Are my instructions, explanations and questions clear and appropriate for pupils' needs?
5 Do I use a variety of question types and distribute these widely throughout the class?
6 Is my general manner confident, relaxed, self-assured and purposeful, and one that is conducive to generating an interest in the lesson and providing support and encouragement for learning?
7 Does my lesson take account of any particular needs of individual pupils, including any special educational needs?
8 Are resources and materials used to good effect?
9 Do I carefully monitor the progress of the lesson and the progress of pupils' learning to ensure that the learning activities are effectively fostering the learning outcomes I intend?
10 Does my general standard of presentation indicate to pupils my respect and care for their learning?

4 Lesson management

Teaching a class of 30 pupils requires a whole range of management and organisational skills if sufficient order necessary for pupil learning is to be maintained. In many ways, I think the task of teaching is rather like the act one sometimes sees on a stage where a person has to spin plates on top of several canes simultaneously. To do this successfully requires the performer to set new plates spinning while occasionally returning to those plates that have slowed down and are near to falling off, for a booster spin. In the same way, successful lesson management requires you to keep switching attention and action between several activities to ensure that pupils' learning proceeds smoothly.

The key task facing you as a teacher is to elicit and sustain pupils' involvement in the learning experience throughout a lesson which will lead to the learning outcomes you intend. At any one time you are likely to have several demands pressing on you for action. For example, you may be dealing with a pupil having problems with the task in hand, then become aware that another pupil needs an item of equipment, also notice another pupil is staring out of the window apparently day-dreaming, and be approached by another pupil who wants some work checked.

Lesson management essentially refers to those skills involved in managing and organising the learning activities such that you maximise pupils' productive involvement in the lesson as much as possible (Dean, 2000; Haydn, 2007; Kyriacou, 1997). Given the large size and range of ability of most classes, this is no mean task! Research based on classroom observation and interviews with beginning and experienced teachers has identified how a successful lesson hinges on certain key lesson management skills.

Paradoxically, watching successful experienced teachers in action tends to provide student teachers with little explicit guidance on successful lesson management skills, since such teachers make everything look too easy. It is only when such teaching is contrasted with that of teachers where problems arise, that the differences in what they do become evident, and the skills used by successful lesson managers can be described.

Beginnings, transitions and endings

One of the key areas of lesson management concerns the skills used in beginning a lesson, handling the transitions within the lesson between activities (say, moving from group work to whole-class discussion) and bringing a lesson to a successful ending.

Beginning punctually

The two most important aspects concerning the beginning of the lesson are punctuality and mental set. It is important for the lesson to start punctually, i.e. fairly soon after the time formally timetabled for its start. This requires that both you and your pupils have arrived for the lesson in good time. Ideally, it is a great help if you can be in the classroom first, to greet pupils as they arrive and to ensure that pupils enter the classroom in an orderly fashion and settle down quickly. Certainly you should convey to pupils that lateness is not acceptable without good excuse.

The first few minutes of a lesson is usually a period of dead time during which pupils settle down, books may be distributed, or you may check material or notes. If possible, you can use this time to good effect by having a social exchange with one or two pupils, or deal with some matters outstanding from a previous lesson, such as a pupil's overdue homework. Once you are happy that everyone has arrived, you need to signal that the lesson itself is ready to begin. This is probably the most important moment in the lesson. It signals the moment that pupils are to pay attention and begin their involvement in the lesson. A clear explicit signal, perhaps saying 'Okay everyone' or 'Pay attention now', is required. It is immensely important for pupils to start paying attention immediately. If you are not happy that all pupils are paying attention, you should indicate this. Trying to continue with the start of a lesson when a few pupils are not paying attention often acts as a signal for others to do likewise in future.

Establishing a positive mental set

Most lessons begin with the topic in hand or with some short activity that needs to be dealt with first, such as comments on homework, or some comment about equipment or materials that everyone should have ready. Whether you start with the topic itself or some other activity, it is important to stand centre-stage, at the front of the room, and to use a clear voice, eye contact and scanning, to ensure everyone is paying attention. A pause followed by a stare at someone not paying attention is often sufficient to signal this.

Once you begin to introduce the topic in hand for the lesson, you need to think about how to elicit and sustain pupils' interest. The best way to do this is to convey in your tone of voice and general manner, a sense of curiosity and excitement, and a sense of purposefulness about what is to follow. Two useful techniques are to establish a link with previous work (e.g. 'Now, you remember last week we looked at . . .') or to pose some questions (e.g. 'Can anybody tell me what the word energy means?'). Such techniques help to establish a positive mental set towards the lesson, i.e. an attitude of mind in which the pupil prepares to devote attention and mental effort towards the activities you set up. A successful introduction to a lesson, which establishes a positive mental set, makes it far easier to sustain learning as the lesson unfolds.

Another aspect of establishing this mental set is to check that every pupil is ready and prepared for the start of the lesson. Are there still pupils with bags on the desk, or standing up talking to each other, or looking for an exercise book that was not handed back? One of the skills involved here is deciding whether to hold up the start of the lesson and chivvy pupils to settle down quickly (e.g. 'Hurry up now, I can still see bags on desks') or whether, if you simply start, pupils will quickly pay attention.

Once a routine for a quick and smooth start to lessons has been well established, you can normally relax the formality of the start, as pupils will quickly respond. However, it is useful from time to time to re-emphasise the procedure and expectations to ensure that they continue to operate well. At the same time, you need to check that you are ready and prepared for the start of the lesson. Are the materials you intend to use readily to hand, has the diagram you wish pupils to talk about been drawn on the board, are the copies of the worksheets to be used ready for distribution? A state of readiness on your part will contribute to your own mental set and this will in turn influence the mental set of pupils.

It is well established that giving pupils 'advanced organisers' at the start of a lesson can be helpful. Advanced organisers refers to ways in which the teacher alerts pupils to how the content and activities of the lesson can be organised and related to their previous knowledge and understanding. However, it appears that explicitly sharing with pupils the learning objectives for the lesson at the start can also have a positive impact on the quality of their work. A study by Seidel *et al.* (2005) indicated that in lessons where the pupils were given a clear idea of the lesson goals, the pupils characterised the lesson as providing a more supportive classroom climate for their learning and they made greater progress in their learning as indicated by their subsequent attainment test scores.

Smooth transitions

The notion of 'smoothness' is helpful when considering whether a lesson has started smoothly and whether there has been a smooth transition between activities (Kounin, 1970). This can best be described by contrasting it with the notion of 'jerkiness'. Jerkiness would be evident if the teacher had to repeat instructions because pupils had not heard or were confused by what was said, or if, having begun a new activity, the teacher kept referring back to the previous activity.

The worst form of jerkiness is attempting to start an activity only to find that some prior activity needed to be undertaken first, and as a result of this needing to stop the activity and change to the prior activity. An example of this would be having to tell pupils who had started working through a worksheet, that they should have been told to read a passage in their textbook first. This not only interrupts the pupils, but makes them feel that their efforts have been wasted through the teacher's poor planning and lesson management. Effective beginnings and transitions are smooth in the sense of lacking jerkiness. Clearly, from time to time, such jerkiness is inevitable and occurs for good educational reasons, such as if it becomes evident that an unforeseeable learning difficulty has arisen. Nevertheless, skilful teaching tends to be characterised by a minimum of unnecessary and avoidable instances of jerkiness.

Two other aspects of transitions contribute to smoothness. First, the teacher needs to be sensitive to how a lesson is progressing in deciding when to initiate a transition. For example, if pupils seem to be working fairly well at a task but somewhat slower than anticipated, the teacher may well decide that it is better to allow more time for the task to be continued, rather than interrupt the activity before it is completed to move them on to another activity. In some cases this may be crucial. A transition to discussion following group work may be harder to set up effectively if the group work has not continued long enough for the issues or ideas to develop that were to form the basis for the discussion.

The second aspect of transitions worthy of note is deciding when to give instructions to the class as a whole, rather than to individuals. All too often a teacher interrupts a class embarking on a new activity simply to issue a further or elaborated instruction which is only of use to two or three particular pupils. It may well have been better and less disruptive for the teacher to talk to each of those pupils privately. The same pitfall can be associated with issuing a reprimand, which again may disrupt the working of a whole class when simple and silent eye contact might have been more effective and less disruptive.

The key point to bear in mind about transitions is that care and attention in setting up a sequence of activities in which pupils are working steadily are just as important as the effort you put into dealing with the content of the learning activities.

Ending the lesson

The ending of lessons can usefully include a few words of praise about the work covered and some conclusions or summary about what was achieved. There are three important issues of management relating to endings. First, a lesson should end on time, neither early, nor, except for special reasons, late. Good time management is one of the skills that pupils will reasonably expect you to have. Ending early can imply a lack of concern about the worthwhileness of using all the time available. Should some time be available at the end of the lesson, this can usefully be spent reviewing or probing the topic covered. Ending late can imply that you lack the organisational skills to marshal the activities, and will deprive you of the opportunity to finish the lesson in a well-ordered and unhurried fashion. Most pupils will naturally resent lessons running over time on a regular basis.

A second management issue is the procedure for getting pupils ready for the end of the lesson. This may involve collecting books and equipment, giving feedback on the work done, and setting homework or other action needed before the next lesson. While this should be done in good time, you also need to ensure that some pupils do not start to pack away too early or before you have signalled that they may do so.

Third, the exit from the classroom should be well ordered. If necessary, it should be controlled, with you dismissing groups of pupils at a time, rather than allowing a rushed exit, until such time as pupils are used to making a well-ordered exit from the classroom without your explicit control.

Maintaining pupils' involvement

Once the lesson is under way, your main task is to maintain pupils' attention, interest and involvement in the learning activities. The task is *not,* however, one of simply keeping pupils busy. There may be a number of activities that you could set up that would effectively keep pupils busy, but they may not be effectively promoting the learning you intend. What makes lesson management skills so sophisticated is the task of setting up activities that are both educationally effective and maintain pupils' involvement.

While the two should go together, it is easy to find some activities erring too far towards only the latter. Skilful lesson management is primarily a question of getting a good balance between the learning potential of an activity and its degree of sustaining pupils' involvement. Since learning cannot occur without involvement, a danger facing teachers is to be uncritical about the quality of learning that occurs when they have successfully maintained a high level of pupil involvement. Nevertheless, at the same time one needs to bear in mind that the learning outcomes which teachers try to achieve include the development of study skills, organisational skills and sustained concentration by pupils. These can usefully be fostered by lengthy periods of working without interaction with the teacher. Hence a teacher may well choose to use an activity that can sustain high pupil involvement for a long period primarily as a means to foster such skills.

Skills in lesson management

An analysis of documents and reports produced by the DfES and Ofsted cover a numbers of skills involved in effective lesson management (e.g. DfES, 2003a,b, 2004a; Ofsted 2002, 2006), although some of these clearly overlap with issues of lesson presentation covered in the previous chapter. In particular these focus on the need to be able to use teaching methods that sustain the momentum of pupils' work and keep all pupils engaged through:

- stimulating their intellectual curiosity, communicating enthusiasm for the subject being taught, fostering pupils' enthusiasm and maintaining their motivation
- structuring information well, including outlining content and aims, signalling transitions and summarising key points as the lesson progresses
- clear instruction and demonstration, and accurate, well-paced explanation
- effective questioning which matches the pace and direction of the lesson and ensures that pupils take part
- listening carefully to pupils, analysing their responses and responding constructively in order to take pupils' learning forward
- providing opportunities for pupils to consolidate their knowledge and maximising opportunities, both in the classroom and through setting well-focused homework, to reinforce and develop what has been learned
- setting high expectations for all pupils notwithstanding individual differences, including gender, and cultural and linguistic backgrounds.

In addition, the TDA (2007) QTS standards include a reference to the need for student teachers to be able to manage the learning of individuals, groups and whole classes, modifying their teaching to suit the stage of the lesson.

Monitoring pupils' progress

Overall, the most important skill involved in maintaining pupils' involvement is that of carefully monitoring pupils' progress. This should be done actively, through circulating around the room and asking probing questions, and passively, by having well-established routines whereby pupils are encouraged to ask for help. Both active and passive monitoring is important. As a result of such monitoring, key decisions may be made about how best to sustain pupils' involvement. Such decisions may relate to the needs of one or two particular pupils or to the needs of the class as a whole.

Pace and flow of the lesson

If pupils' attention or interest in the lesson seems to be on the wane, a number of possible reasons may account for this. It may be that a particular activity is being employed for too long (most commonly a long exposition). Alternatively, it may be that the general pace and flow of the lesson is either too fast or too slow.

If the pace of activities (be it exposition, group work, worksheets or reading tasks) is too fast, pupils will simply wilt or find that they are missing important points or ideas. If the pace is too slow, pupils' minds can easily start to wander. Indeed, an important aspect of maintaining the correct pace during exposition involves having a sense of how long to dwell on each particular point for understanding to occur and not spending too long dwelling on minor points or points already well taken.

In addition, maintaining a good pace also involves avoiding unnecessary interruptions to the flow of the lesson. For example, if while explaining a task, you stop in order to get a pencil for a pupil, or to find a map you need to refer to, or to reprimand a pupil, the flow of the lesson will be interrupted. A useful lesson management skill is that of dealing with the demands that arise, or postponing dealing with them, so that they are not allowed to interrupt the flow of the lesson. For example, if while explaining a task you notice two pupils talking, you may continue your explanation while looking at the two pupils concerned, or, if necessary, move towards them. This would enable the flow of the lesson to continue while dealing with the problem. This skill is sometimes referred to as 'overlapping', i.e. dealing with two or more tasks at the same time.

Another example of overlapping is the teacher's ability to monitor pupils' progress and behaviour while giving individual help to a particular pupil. A skilful teacher is able to listen to a pupil reading aloud or give help with some number work, for example, while at the same time periodically scanning the classroom and listening to the background noise to pick out any behaviour giving concern. This involves quickly

You have to be able to do a wide variety of things at the same time

switching attention between your interaction with the particular pupil and what else is going on in the classroom. Indeed, a particular pitfall for beginning teachers is to become so engrossed in giving individual help and attention that they fail to monitor what else is happening. In contrast, experienced teachers are much more skilful in their attention switching.

Withitness

The general awareness of what is going on in the classroom is commonly referred to as 'withitness' (Kounin, 1970). Experienced teachers are adept at picking up cues and signals which indicate to them what is going on. A quick downward glance by a pupil in the back row, or a furtive look at a neighbour, or simply taking slightly too long to walk to a seat, can all be picked up by a teacher as signalling the onset of possible misbehaviour.

Beginning teachers are often so overwhelmed by all the demands of classroom life that they find it difficult to pick up such signals. With increasing experience, which gradually makes the unfamiliar familiar, the teacher becomes better able to pick up and monitor subtle cues of this type. As such, it is useful for beginning teachers to consciously make an effort to scan the classroom periodically and monitor general behaviour, to see if anything gives concern. It is also useful to bear in mind the times when such monitoring is vulnerable. As well as when giving individual help, times when your back is turned to the classroom while writing on the board or looking in cupboards may interrupt your monitoring. A useful technique when writing on the board is to face sideways or to glance back at the class regularly, and to listen carefully to any background noise.

Interestingly, the importance of lesson-managing skills relating to transition, overlapping and withitness, was highlighted in a seminal study by Kounin (1970), in which he compared the videotaped classroom behaviour of teachers who were regarded as having few discipline problems with teachers having frequent problems. What was particularly noticeable was that the former's relative success largely stemmed from them simply being more effective lesson managers, rather than anything to do with how they dealt with pupil misbehaviour itself. Research on teaching skills, including my own (e.g. Kyriacou and McKelvey, 1985), indicates that experienced teachers are generally very skilful in these three important aspects of their classroom practice.

Managing pupils' time

Pupils' involvement in the lesson can also be facilitated if they are given a clear idea of how much time and effort they are expected to devote to particular tasks or activities. For example, if you ask pupils to copy a map into their exercise books and answer three questions relating to the map, some pupils may rush the task, anticipating that ten minutes should be sufficient time, and others may assume the task is intended to last half-an-hour. If you indicate that the task should take about 20 minutes, it will help pupils to tailor their effort to the time available.

There can, of course, sometimes be a danger in encouraging pupils to perhaps take longer than they need. In general, however, it helps to ensure that some pupils do not work slowly only to find they are halfway through a task when you want pupils to move on to another activity. It also helps to maintain attention and interest, since they have a clear sense that another activity is shortly to follow. This also helps to break the lesson up into more attractive chunks of time.

Giving supportive feedback

Constructive and helpful feedback also needs to be given to pupils to support and encourage further progress (Black *et al.,* 2003; Gardner, 2006). Such feedback is not only of practical use to pupils in identifying problems or indicating successful work, but also conveys to pupils that their progress is being carefully monitored and that you care about such progress. Such regular feedback thus offers a periodic boost to the motivation and effort.

The skill of offering such feedback is a fairly complex one that needs time and practice to develop. You need to be able to identify the nature of the pupil's problem. Simply indicating a 'correct' method or answer may not be enough to give the pupil the insight necessary. You also need to be able to offer feedback in a way that is unthreatening, since once a pupil feels anxious, it is harder for the pupil to follow what is being said. This requires the use of a sympathetic tone of voice, and locating the problem in the task or activity, rather than in the pupil. In other words, it is better to say 'In this type of question, it is a good idea to start by taking careful note of the information given in the diagram', rather than 'You should have been more careful in your approach'. The former statement is task-focused, whereas the latter locates the fault or blame with the pupil. This sensitivity to pupils' feelings is now widely appreciated as being an important aspect of the skill involved in providing supportive feedback. Indeed, a number of studies of pupils' views of their teachers have reported that the teacher's capacity to empathise was one of the most valued teacher qualities cited by the pupils (Cullingford, 2003).

Giving individual feedback privately to each pupil in a fairly large class is clearly going to be demanding, and attempting to do this will almost certainly distract you from other important tasks. Consequently you need to maintain a good balance between giving individual feedback and other strategies, including giving feedback to the whole class, or enabling pupils to correct their own or each other's work. These other techniques help to ensure that feedback occurs regularly and with sufficient speed to improve the quality of work and learning. However, you do need to ensure that such techniques are used sensitively, given the emotional consequences of identifying failure.

It is thus a good idea to circulate around the classroom whilst pupils are engaged in a task, and to give them ongoing feedback on their work in an informal manner. You can take these opportunities to use the technique of 'scaffolding': this is where the teacher helps a pupil who is in difficulty by drawing their attention to the key features of the task and through dialogue with the pupil, gradually guiding the pupil towards the understanding they need in order to complete the task successfully.

Adjusting your lesson plans

Careful monitoring of pupils' progress and giving feedback also enables you to consider how best the lesson ought to proceed in the light of its success to date and any problems encountered. While lesson plans are important, all teachers will need to tailor the development of the lesson to the needs of the moment. Part of successful lesson management involves making whatever adjustments to your original plans for the lesson are necessary. In doing so, however, always ensure that you have a good feel as to how the class as a whole is progressing. Clearly, just because one or two pupils are finding the work too easy or too difficult or lacking interest, this should not be taken as a signal that this is generally true for most of the class. Once you get to know a class fairly well, however, it becomes possible to make useful inferences from the behaviour of just a handful of pupils. If, for example, two or three pupils who normally find the work in hand difficult are suddenly racing through a particular task, you may well be fairly certain that most pupils in the class are going to complete the task quickly without the need for you to check too widely for confirmation.

Handling the logistics of classroom life

Lesson management skills are essential if the learning activities you set up are to take place with sufficient order for learning to occur. Almost any task or activity can lead to chaos unless you give some thought to the organisation of how and when pupils are to do what is required of them. Organised control over the logistics of classroom life, whether it be how pupils answer questions, collect equipment from cupboards, or form themselves into small groups, requires explicit direction from you, at least until the procedures you expect are followed as a matter of routine.

Social demand tasks

Research on teachers' management effectiveness indicates that every learning activity involves a 'social demand task'. This social demand task might be, for example, who can talk to whom, about what, where, when, in what ways and for what purpose. Such research highlights the importance of how teachers indicate to pupils what is required of them, and facilitate the smooth and effective running of the activity. Indeed, with the increasing variety of learning activities used, effective lesson management skills need to be applied to a host of very different types of activities to deal with the social demand task involved in each. This has become increasingly evident in looking at the different ways in which ICT use in the classroom has generated new types of social demands which teachers have to manage skilfully.

Group work

Setting up group-work activities involves a number of decisions about the logistics of their organisation (Jaques, 2000). First, there is the question of the size of the group and how groups are to be formed. If you have a task which, ideally, involves four pupils, you need to think about how the groups of four are to be created, and what to do if there are one or more pupils left over, or, indeed, one or two pupils whom no one wants in their group.

A second question concerns the nature of the task. Is it clear exactly what the task involves, who will undertake which roles, and how and what is to be produced? A clear instruc-tion, such as 'At the end, each group will give a list of the four most important factors involved, in order of importance' is clearer than simply getting each group to discuss the factors involved. Often, it is useful to write the task on the board or on a briefing handout issued to each pupil or group. You may wish to let each group decide who should report back at the end, or name a pupil from each group to do this (the latter is useful in ensuring that certain pupils are given the experience of doing this).

A third aspect of group work concerns your monitoring role. While close monitoring is usually desirable, particularly in checking that everyone is clear about the task, your presence may have an inhibiting effect on group discussion and, as such, it is often better to spend only a short while with each group to check that everything is in order, rather than to sit in for any length of time.

Fourth, clear time management directions are crucial to most group-work activities. It is useful to say how long each group has for the task as a whole, and also how much time they may spend on any stages that make up the task. One last aspect concerning group work is the need to help pupils develop the skills involved in successful group work. Pupils need to develop a number of skills to use group work to good effect, and feedback and guidance from you on good practice can help such skills to develop.

These points are well reflected in a review of the literature by Kutnick *et al.* (2005) which looked at the research evidence on how to use group work effectively. Their report highlighted the importance of ensuring that: (i) the task is broken down so that pupils can assess their own progress; (ii) the group is supported in working independently by providing hints about the task and also about group working; and (iii) the timing for each component is made explicit.

Practicals

Practicals of any sort present a number of logistical problems, in part because you need to co-ordinate your management of pupils and materials with the sequence and speed of the practical itself. In a science practical, for example, there may be a 20-minute period during which some effect is developing; this period can be actively used to explore with pupils what is going on and to probe their thinking and the care they are taking to observe and record any changes.

Another common problem regarding practicals may arise if certain equipment needs to be shared. Again, a strict rota for the use of such equipment or a procedure to ensure its speedy use and return, can make a large difference to reducing unproductive time. During practicals, there are often times when bottlenecks can occur, such as when everyone wants to collect or return equipment, or perhaps wash apparatus. Simple rules, such as only allowing one pupil from each group to collect apparatus, can help prevent such problems.

Using ICT

Unless you can arrange for all pupils to have ready access to the ICT equipment they need to use at the same time, such as booking an ICT suite, you will need to organise a rota of some sort. One point about pairs – or occasionally a small group of three pupils – working together when using ICT is that it is useful in most cases to group together pupils of similar ability, unless you explicitly wish one pupil to act as a tutor. With other types of group work, friendship groupings seem to work well, unless there is a clear educational rationale for forming the groups on the basis of similar ability or in some other way.

Managing pupil movement and noise

Two of the most important aspects of effective management skills are maintaining adequate control over the movement of pupils around the classroom and keeping the degree of noise generated at an appropriate level. In both cases, part of the difficulty lies in there being no fixed acceptable standard; what may be acceptable to one teacher in one context, may not be regarded as acceptable to another teacher in another context. Furthermore, problems over movement and noise can arise simply as a result of pupils being actively engaged in the tasks at hand and not because of any deliberate attempt by pupils to be troublesome.

Pupil movement

We have already touched on some aspects of pupil movement in the classroom earlier in this chapter, such as entering and leaving the room, and collecting equipment. In addition to these, there are some occasions which require particular attention. The first of these involves giving out books at the start of or during the lesson. It is certainly important to issue books rather than allow pupils to collect them from a central point. Often, it is more efficient for you to ask two or three pupils to issue books, rather than do it yourself, unless you feel that distributing books yourself will provide a useful social function or enable you to have a few pertinent words with some pupils. If pupils are issuing the books, ensure that they do so sensibly and with care.

The second aspect concerns any mass movement of pupils; this always requires careful control. Whilst useful routines can be established, there are occasions when you need to organise a somewhat unusual or novel arrangement. For example, you may wish to

Managing pupils' movement

devise a role-play activity that requires all the classroom furniture, apart from eight chairs, to be moved towards the edge of the classroom. Any complicated manoeuvre of this sort requires prior thought if it is to proceed smoothly. A clear sequence of tasks and who needs to do what is essential.

The third aspect involves establishing your expectations concerning when pupils may leave their seat. Despite new forms of teaching and learning, most pupils will spend the majority of their time in their seats. The management of pupils being out of their seat during periods of work when pupils are expected to work at their desk is important. The normal expectation during such activities is that pupils remain at their desk until given explicit permission to move, unless certain well-established routines allowing movement without explicit permission are followed. In such circumstances it is useful to ensure that only a handful of pupils at any one time are out of their seats, or away from their work area; it becomes much harder to monitor pupils' progress if several pupils appear to be wandering about, even if their purposes are legitimate. This is one reason why teachers often set an upper limit on how many pupils are allowed to queue up at the teacher's desk. Being out of one's seat for some pupils also acts as a break from their work, and they may feel like extending this break longer than necessary, and may also, as a result, start to disturb others. This needs careful monitoring.

Pupil noise

Managing the general level of noise is also an important management skill. Every teacher develops their own standard of acceptable level of noise. The key thing here is to be reasonably consistent, so that pupils have a clear idea of your expectations. If the level of background noise during an activity appears to be too high, it is useful to give specific feedback on the work practice you require, rather than make a general complaint that the noise is too high. Thus, for example, it is better to say 'You can talk to your neighbour, but not to other pupils' or 'Try to ensure that only one person in each group is speaking at a time', than simply to say 'The noise level is too high' or 'Less noise please'.

It is also worth planning the activities to ensure that noise levels are not disruptive. For example, in a science practical looking at sound as a form of energy, clear instructions on how the apparatus or equipment is to be used can prevent problems occurring through unnecessarily high noise levels. Indeed, the opportunity to make a lot of noise legitimately is too tempting for many pupils to resist. At the same time, it must be recognised that a certain level of noise is, of course, acceptable and desirable, and that enthusiastic and excited contributions by pupils need to be harnessed to good effect rather than squashed. Clearly, a balance that ensures sufficient order is what is needed.

Some studies, however, have indicated that the teacher's management of noise can sometimes become an end in itself. Given that the noise level of a class is often taken as an indicator of the teacher's level of control, many teachers are very sensitive about their classroom noise level, particularly if they feel it may be heard by colleagues or interfere with colleagues' lessons. Indeed, beginning teachers often feel themselves to be under particular pressure to control the noise level of their classes lest it conveys to colleagues that they lack control. As a result, some teachers may make more frequent use of certain learning activities because they will help sustain periods of quiet work by pupils despite the fact that other learning activities might be more effective for the learning outcomes intended but have more potential to generate noise. Indeed, the reluctance that some teachers have to make greater use of group work is related to the greater level of noise such activity typically generates.

Movement and noise as constraints on your teaching

While the management of movement and noise is important, you do need to be on your guard as to whether, as indicated above, you are allowing management considerations to have too great an influence on your choice of effective learning activities. Skilful lesson management involves an interplay between the different constraints within which you operate. Clearly, you need to ensure that a role-play activity involving a lot of movement and noise does not disturb another class, or that one pupil's excitement does not lead to other pupils being constantly interrupted when they are speaking. At the same time, you need to ensure that the learning activity does facilitate and encourage pupils' attention, interest and involvement in the lesson, and that this is not unduly inhibited by management strategies that could be usefully relaxed to good effect.

One of the dilemmas facing teachers is that they may feel better able to manage certain types of lessons, and as a result are reluctant to use other types of learning activities. This reluctance may persist despite the fact that certain curriculum developments have made the need for such change essential. This was evident, for example, in studies of how teachers' classroom practice has been influenced by the introduction of the National Curriculum, with many teachers expressing hostility and resistance towards the need for them to change their established practice. Indeed, senior managers in some schools welcomed the National Curriculum because it made it easier for them to put pressure on colleagues to change certain aspects of their classroom practice by externalising the source of the need for change: 'Your practice has got to change, not because it's my idea, but because the National Curriculum requires it'. This type of pressure for change was also very evident when the National Numeracy Strategy and the National Literacy Strategy were introduced.

In thinking about your own classroom practice, you should not be wary of setting up activities that may involve more than usual movement or noise, as long as this is well managed and to good purpose. Some years ago a well-known headteacher remarked that effective teaching could sometimes be described as 'organised chaos'. On the one hand, I think that there is some truth in this description in so far as some effective lessons may well appear to have such a quality. On the other hand, there can at times be a danger in thinking that certain activities are so worthwhile in their own right, particularly in terms of the extent to which they may offer pupils a fair measure of control over their work, that the need to maintain sufficient order and control for effective learning can be relaxed. While I am a strong advocate of using a variety of learning activities, particularly active learning methods, there is always a need to ensure that effective learning is going on, and to provide the conditions that will facilitate this. Again, what is required here is an appropriate balance between the management strategies used and the type of learning outcomes you intend, most notably if the learning outcomes are in terms of developing pupils' own skills to organise themselves.

Further reading

Haydn, T. (2007) *Managing Pupil Behaviour: Key Issues in Teaching and Learning*. London: Routledge. This book contains insightful and helpful advice on lesson management.

Kerry, T. and Wilding, M. (2004). *Effective Classroom Teacher: Developing the Skills You Need in Today's Classroom*. London: Pearson. An excellent overview of the facets involved in being an effective teacher and the teaching skills that underpin these.

Kyriacou, C. (1997) *Effective Teaching in Schools,* 2nd edn. Cheltenham: Nelson Thornes. This book looks at the theory and practice involved in effective teaching and links the teaching skills involved in effective teaching with the wider research context.

Muijs, D. and Reynolds, D. (2005) *Effective Teaching: Evidence and Practice,* 2nd edn. London: Sage. A good overview of effective teaching which takes careful account of research evidence.

Key questions about your lesson management

1 Does my lesson start smoothly and promptly, and induce a positive mental set among pupils?
2 Does the management of the lesson help to elicit and maintain pupils' attention, interest and motivation?
3 Is the pace and flow of the lesson maintained at an appropriate level and are transitions between activities well managed?
4 Do I carefully monitor the progress of pupils so that the effectiveness of the lesson is maintained by giving individual help or making modifications and adjustments to the development of the lesson, as appropriate?
5 Do I give clear guidance and direction on what is expected of pupils during each activity, and manage their time and effort, in relation to their involvement in and the sequencing of the various activities, to good effect?
6 Do I make effective use of the various materials, resources and teaching aids, so that pupils' time is not wasted waiting for equipment to be set up or materials distributed?
7 Do I organise and control the logistics of classroom life, such as how pupils answer questions, collect equipment or form into groups, so that the order necessary for learning to occur is maintained?
8 In particular, do I use effective management strategies in handling pupil movement and the general level of noise?
9 Is the feedback conveyed to pupils about their progress helpful and constructive, and does it encourage further progress?
10 Do my lessons end effectively, in terms of ending on time, drawing the topic of the lesson to an appropriate conclusion, and having a well-ordered exit by pupils from the classroom?

5 Classroom climate

The classroom climate established by the teacher can have a major impact on pupils' motivation and attitudes towards learning (Cullingford, 2003; Pollard *et al.*, 2000). As such, the skills involved in establishing a positive classroom climate are of immense importance. Indeed, a study by Day *et al.* (2006, 2007) found that having the skills to establish a positive classroom climate, and in particular to establish a positive relationship with pupils, was seen by teachers to lie at the heart of their view of themselves as effective teachers.

Establishing a positive classroom climate

The type of classroom climate generally considered to best facilitate pupil learning is one that is described as being purposeful, task-oriented, relaxed, warm, supportive and has a sense of order. Such a climate facilitates learning, in essence, by establishing and maintaining positive attitudes and motivation by pupils towards the lesson. In analysing the skills involved in setting up a positive classroom climate, it is clear that the climate largely derives from the values that are implicit and pervade the lesson – simply that pupils and their learning are of immense importance. Interestingly, a study by Kaplan *et al.* (2002) found that the level of disruptive behaviour by pupils tended to be higher in those classrooms where the pupils felt that the demonstration of ability and doing better than others was the dominant value compared with classrooms where the pupils felt that the dominant value was learning, understanding and improving one's own performance.

Purposeful and task-oriented

A purposeful and task-oriented ethos stems largely from the way in which the teacher emphasises the need to make steady progress with the learning in hand. An important aspect of this derives from your insistence that time must not be wasted. Hence, a prompt start to the lesson, close monitoring of pupils' progress, and careful attention to organisational matters, all help to ensure a smooth flow to the lesson and maintenance of pupil involvement. Where teachers allow minor matters or avoidable organisational problems to interrupt the flow of the lesson, a message is conveyed to pupils that the learning is not of such immense importance that it warrants more care to ensure that it is not interrupted. Certainly, conveying in your tone of voice or, even worse, adding a preamble to a topic that it is not particularly worthwhile, will undermine the creation of a purposeful and task-oriented ethos. Ending a lesson early is likely to have the same effect.

Overall, a purposeful and task-oriented emphasis can usefully be described as a 'business-like' style of presentation. This is characterised by pupils' acceptance of the teacher's authority to organise and manage the learning activities, and a pervading expectation by the teacher and pupils that positive effort will be made by pupils to undertake the work in hand and that good progress will be made.

A very important aspect of establishing such positive expectations by pupils is the need to ensure that they have self-respect and self-esteem. This can, in part, be fostered by providing realistic opportunities for success, and helpful support and encouragement, whenever pupils experience difficulties. Learning is an emotionally high-risk activity and failure is often extremely painful. Prolonged experience of failure or deprecating remarks by a teacher about pupils' low attainment can have devastating consequences for pupils' self-esteem. As a result, quite naturally, such pupils are likely to withdraw from making further efforts as a means of protecting themselves from further pain (in effect, if I am not trying, my lack of success is simply my choice).

Relaxed, warm and supportive

A relaxed, warm and supportive ethos stems largely from the style and manner of the relationship you establish with the pupils. Being relaxed yourself, and in particular, dealing with any pupil misbehaviour calmly, helps pupils to relax too. This better enables pupils to develop curiosity and interest in the learning activities.

Warmth can best be thought of as conveying to pupils a sense that you care for them and their learning personally, partly out of your affection for them as individuals. This is conveyed in the way you deal with individual pupils. Simply saying, after giving individual help, 'Have you got that now?' in a sympathetic and caring tone of voice (rather than in a harsh and admonishing tone), can do much to convey this sense of warmth. Pye (1988), in his analysis of skilful teaching, used the phrase 'solicitous tenderness' to describe the mixture of warmth, reassurance, kindness and tact shown by skilful teachers in how they handle interactions with pupils.

Being supportive involves the efforts you make to help and encourage pupils to meet the demands made on them and, in particular, to deal with the difficulties they encounter in a situation where they need further assistance rather than being reprimanded. However, you do need to be aware of the fact that too readily providing individual help and support may encourage some pupils to rely on such help rather than to make the appropriate effort to pay attention during whole-class teaching or to work things out for themselves. In giving supportive feedback, you can usefully help pupils to develop study skills by indicating how paying attention earlier or using certain strategies in approaching their work will enable them to meet the demands made on them. In the context of establishing a positive classroom climate, such feedback can be a useful part of offering support.

A sense of order

A final aspect of a positive classroom climate is the need to establish a sense of order. Clearly, a sense of order can be established in many different ways. What is advocated here is that in order to contribute to a positive classroom climate, such order needs to arise out of and complement the other features considered in establishing a purposeful, task-oriented, relaxed, warm and supportive ethos. Such order will thus be based on effective lesson presentation and lesson management skills and on a relationship with pupils based on mutual respect and rapport.

Studies of classroom climate

A number of studies looking at effective teaching and effective schools have focused on the notion of climate or ethos (Muijs and Reynolds, 2005). These include some particularly interesting research that has focused on the wider notion of the 'learning environment' of which the classroom climate is a part. For example, Fraser (2002) has identified several aspects of the learning environment that relate to classroom climate, such as:

- *involvement:* the extent to which pupils show attentive interest, participate in discussions, do additional work and enjoy the class
- *equity:* the extent to which pupils are treated equally and fairly by the teacher
- *differentiation:* the extent to which teachers cater for pupils differently on the basis of ability, rates of learning, and interests
- *responsibility for own learning:* the extent to which pupils perceive themselves as being in charge of their learning process, motivated by constant feedback and affirmation.

A number of writers have also highlighted the importance of the classroom climate being 'inclusive' or 'incorporative': the extent to which all pupils in the class feel themselves to be a full participant in class activities and to be a valued member of the class (Campbell *et al.,* 2004; Watkins, 2005). The opposite of this would be a class where some pupils feel marginalised and feel the work they do in the class is not valued. The notion of 'inclusive teaching' also features strongly in the Every Child Matters agenda developed by the DfES to promote pupil achievement in schools (Cheminais, 2006). The notion of inclusive teaching originally developed as part of a consideration of good classroom practice regarding the inclusion of pupils with special educational needs, but is now used much more widely to refer to the ways in which all pupils in the class can feel engaged and involved in classroom activities and tasks, as a way of combating the feelings of disaffection or isolation amongst pupils whose background or circumstances make them vulnerable.

Studies of classroom climate have provided a wealth of evidence to support the importance of a positive classroom climate in facilitating pupil learning, and are in line with the judgements expressed in a series of HMI and Ofsted reports dealing with aspects of skilful teaching and good classroom practice.

Interestingly, a number of studies have also noted how important the first few lessons with a new class are in establishing a positive classroom climate. Wragg (2005), for example, compared the behaviour of experienced teachers with that of student teachers during their first few lessons with a new class, and noted that experienced teachers:

- were more confident, warm and friendly
- were more business-like
- were more stimulating

- were more mobile
- made greater use of eye contact
- made greater use of humour
- were clearer about their classroom rules
- better established their presence and authority.

These are all features which helped the experienced teachers to establish fairly quickly a positive working climate for the school year ahead.

There is also research evidence to indicate that a positive classroom climate is more likely to be established by the use of a learner-centred teaching style. A study by Opdenakker and Van Damme (2006) identified seven key features of a learner-centred teaching style which enabled teachers to develop a positive classroom climate:

- the use of differentiated activities and material
- undertaking activities to help problem pupils
- active pupil participation in lessons
- discussing pupil and class affairs with other teachers using the assessment of pupils to direct one's own teaching
- an orientation towards the development of the person(ality) of the pupils
- establishing a personal relationship with pupils based on trust.

In recent years the use of whole-class interactive teaching 'with pace' has been advocated as a way in which teachers can establish a positive classroom climate. The use of ICT has also been seen as a means of sustaining pupils' engagement in lessons. The use of interactive whiteboards has been seen by many as offering the best of both worlds in combining interactive whole-class teaching with ICT. A study by Smith *et al.* (2006), which looked at the quality of pupil–teacher interaction in lessons using interactive whiteboards in the context of the National Literacy and Numeracy Strategies, found that many teachers were using interactive whiteboards with a traditional type of whole-class teaching. It is clear that using interactive whiteboards 'interactively' requires a high degree of skill by both the teacher and the pupils.

Skills in establishing a positive classroom climate

Given the importance of establishing a positive classroom climate, it is not surprising that descriptions of the skills that need to be displayed by teachers often make a specific reference to these. For example, the TDA (2007) QTS standards include the following elements as a means whereby teachers can establish a positive classroom climate:

- establishing a purposeful and safe learning environment conducive to learning
- having high expectations of pupils including a commitment to ensuring that pupils can achieve their full educational potential
- establishing fair, respectful, trusting, supportive and constructive relationships with pupils
- demonstrating the positive values, attitudes and behaviour they expect from pupils

- supporting and guiding pupils to reflect upon their learning and to identify their learning needs
- knowing how to identify and support pupils whose progress, development or well-being is affected by changes or difficulties in their personal circumstances, and when to refer them to colleagues for specialist support.

Motivating pupils

An essential feature of the teaching skills involved in establishing a positive classroom climate is how best to foster pupils' motivation towards learning. In looking at pupil motivation, a useful distinction can be made between three major influences on pupil motivation in the classroom:

- intrinsic motivation
- extrinsic motivation
- expectation for success.

Influences on pupil motivation

Intrinsic motivation concerns the extent to which pupils engage in an activity to satisfy their curiosity and interest in the topic area being covered, or develop their competence and skills in dealing with the demands made on them, *for their own sake*. All human beings appear to have a natural drive of curiosity and wish to develop competence and skills in various tasks for their own sake, rather than as a means to some other end.

Extrinsic motivation involves engaging in an activity in order to achieve some end or goal that is rewarding and is external to the task itself. Engaging in the activity is thus a means towards some other end (e.g. getting praise from parents or the teacher, an academic qualification, eliciting respect and admiration from fellow pupils, or avoiding some unpleasant consequences of being unsuccessful). Intrinsic and extrinsic motivation are often contrasted with each other, but are not in fact incompatible. Indeed, many pupils have high intrinsic and high extrinsic motivation for engaging in a particular task. For example, they may work hard in their mathematics lessons both because they enjoy doing mathematics and because it is important for them to attain well in order to realise their career aspirations.

Expectation for success concerns the extent to which pupils feel they are likely to succeed at a particular activity. Many pupils will not attempt to make strenuous efforts to succeed at a task they feel is far too difficult for them and they therefore have little hope of succeeding with. Interestingly, however, not all tasks which pupils feel they can easily succeed at may be motivating; tasks that are far too easy may be seen by pupils as not being worthy of making the effort unless there is some explicit reason to do so. Research evidence indicates that the tasks that best elicit pupil motivation are those seen by pupils to be challenging, i.e. difficult but achievable (Brophy, 2004).

Eliciting pupil motivation

The key strategies which teachers can use to elicit pupil motivation are thus concerned with building upon pupils' intrinsic motivation, extrinsic motivation and their

Eliciting pupils' motivation

expectation for success. It is important to note, however, that there are large individual differences between pupils in how and when their intrinsic motivation, extrinsic motivation and expectation for success are elicited.

To a great extent these will be influenced by their experience at home (particularly how much encouragement they receive from parents to be interested in and value school learning and school-related attainment), by their experience in school (particularly their experience of success and failure to date), and by how they perceive teachers' expectations of them and the demands of various tasks. In the context of skilful teaching, the most important factor is to ensure that pupils are supported and encouraged to learn, with high positive expectations being conveyed by the teacher. Such expectations need to be realistic but challenging; they need to convey that the activities are worthwhile and of interest; and, above all, they need to convey that each pupil's progress really does matter.

Building on intrinsic motivation

Strategies that build on pupils' intrinsic motivation include selecting topics that are likely to interest pupils, particularly if they relate to pupils' own experiences. For example, a task on drawing charts could be based on how pupils in the class travelled to school that morning.

Offering choice can also elicit interest. For example, in composing a school newspaper, those interested in sports could compile the sports page. Active involvement and co-operation between pupils also fosters enjoyment. The use of various games has much to offer. Novelty and variety also provides a more stimulating experience. For example, starting off a lesson by producing a shoe box that purports to contain the belongings of a person, and then trying to build up as much information about the person as possible from these belongings, would do this effectively.

Because intrinsic motivation involves a drive towards increasing competence, as well as a curiosity drive, it can also be fostered by providing pupils with regular feedback on how their skills and competence are developing, and drawing to their attention what they can do and understand now compared with before the course of work began.

Building on extrinsic motivation

Strategies that build on pupils' extrinsic motivation include linking effort and success to material rewards and privileges. You must be extremely careful, however, to ensure that the reward or privilege offered is actually one desired by the pupils concerned and does not undermine their intrinsic motivation or alienate those who make an effort but who are not rewarded in this way. For example, offering the opportunity to those who work hard to start their break early, seems to devalue the worthwhileness of the activity; offering a book token to the best piece of project work may again offer far more hurt to those unsuccessful than pleasure to the pupil who wins it.

Other strategies include esteem-related rewards, such as high grades or other forms of recognition for effort and success, although again, if such rewards are overtly competitive, you need to be aware of their possible effect on other pupils. Teacher praise is a very important and powerful motivation, although its effect depends on skilful use. Praise that is explicitly linked to the pupil's efforts and attainment, which conveys sincere pleasure on the teacher's part, and which is used with credibility, is more effective than praise simply offered on a regular basis but lacking these qualities.

Extrinsic motivation can also be highlighted by indicating to pupils the usefulness, relevance and importance of the topic or activity to their needs. These may be their short-term needs, such as academic qualifications or high test scores of attainment, or their long-term needs, such as coping with the demands of adult life successfully or helping to realise their career aspirations.

Building on expectation for success

Strategies that build upon pupils' expectation for success include ensuring that the tasks set are challenging and offer pupils a realistic chance of success, taking into account their ability and previous learning. In particular, you need to try to minimise any unnecessary frustration caused by setting up the activities poorly. This requires close monitoring of pupils' progress once the lesson is under way, together with quick and supportive feedback when a pupil has encountered major difficulties.

Your help and expectations must convey confidence in the pupils and your belief that with appropriate effort they will be successful. When dealing with pupils who lack confidence in themselves as learners, such help and expectations are of crucial importance. It is also important to convey that success lies in their own hands, and that they need to be aware of how they approach tasks, the degree of persistence they have to apply to be successful, and that there is no substitute for a willingness on their part to apply sustained effort.

Your relationships with pupils

A positive classroom climate very much depends on the type of relationship you establish with your pupils. Pupils' learning is most likely to flourish in a climate where this relationship is based on mutual respect and rapport between yourself and your pupils.

Mutual respect and rapport

Mutual respect largely develops from the pupils seeing by your actions that you are a competent teacher, and that you care about their progress by planning and conducting effective lessons and carrying out your various tasks with commitment. In addition, you convey in your dealings with pupils, both during whole-class teaching and in your interactions with individuals, that you respect each pupil as an individual who has individual and personal needs.

Good rapport stems from conveying to pupils that you understand, share and value their perspective, as individuals, on a whole range of matters and experiences, academic, social and personal: for example, expressing sympathy when the local football team is knocked out of a cup competition, praise for a pupil who had performed well in a school play, concern for a pupil who has a bad cold, and excitement that a school trip is near. The development of a positive classroom climate depends on this relationship being two-way: your respect for pupils should be reciprocated in their respect for you, and your understanding of their perspectives reciprocated in their understanding of yours. Nevertheless, as an adult, and given your role, it is up to you to have a major influence in establishing such a harmonious relationship in the classroom.

The skills involved in establishing a climate of mutual respect and rapport are highly prized in schools, as they also have a major impact on the general climate of the school as a whole. They also contribute to the pastoral care role of the teacher, and make it easier for pupils to come to you with their personal problems and difficulties. Indeed, a high proportion of outstanding teachers in inner-city comprehensive schools tend to be very skilful in developing good rapport with potentially difficult and demanding adolescents and, not surprisingly, many of these outstanding teachers have specific pastoral care responsibilities in the school as a result. Pye (1988), interestingly, noticed how skilful teachers were able to convey a personal manner in their interaction with an individual pupil during a private exchange, in which the mutual respect and rapport established was particularly evident. Pye described this as a situation in which the teacher and pupil were 'acknowledging' each other; i.e. they had established a personal relationship that was separate from, and yet still part of, the relationship that the teacher had with the class as a whole.

Acting as a good example

It is also important to be aware of the influence that your behaviour can have on pupils in acting as an example or model for their own behaviour. This identification with the teacher is evident in both the primary and secondary school years. Pupils will expect you to be a good example of the expectations that you convey. If you insist on neat work, your own board work should also be neat. If you expect pupils to act in a civilised manner, you should not lose your temper or use sarcasm to hurt their feelings. If you want pupils to find the work interesting, you should convey interest in the activities yourself. Indeed, in a number of their reports based on school inspections, Ofsted frequently report on the particular importance of the example set by the teacher in establishing a positive ethos in the classroom.

The use of humour

One of the difficulties facing beginning teachers concerns knowing whether, how and when to use humour in the classroom, and the extent to which their relationship with pupils should be friendly. Judicious use of humour and conveying that you have a sense of humour can play a useful part in helping to establish good rapport and a positive classroom climate. Humour can be used to good effect in a whole range of situations, including introducing a light-hearted aspect of the work in hand or making a joke at your own expense (and, if done skilfully, making a joke at the pupil's expense but in a way that enables the pupil to share the joke rather than feel victimised).

Humour can also be used to reassure a pupil who is anxious or in difficulties or to defuse a potential conflict with a pupil about misbehaviour. Conveying that you have a sense of humour is indicated in the way you respond to events that occur with good humour or share with pupils some amusement which they see in a situation. It might be something as simple as how you react to a pupil's aside (e.g. 'Did a division of "minute men" in the American War of Independence consist of three hours' worth?').

Linked with the use of humour is the extent to which you try to establish friendly relations with pupils. Part of establishing good rapport with pupils involves sharing to some extent each other's understanding and perspective on the demands of classroom life and life outside the classroom in general. This will include valuing and respecting each other as individuals and valuing each other's viewpoints. Much of this forms the basis of friendship between individuals. Nevertheless, the classroom is a unique and, to a large extent, a very ritualised environment. To sustain order and control, your relationship with pupils, above all, must be one in which they respect and accept your authority to manage and control what happens in the classroom so that their learning may progress effectively. This means that your manner needs to be competent, business-like and task-oriented. Frequent use of humour, particularly being 'jokey', and trying to act as a friend of equal status, tends to undermine your authority because it does not accord with the ritual of school life and how pupils typically see and react to different aspects of a teacher's manner.

As a result, beginning teachers who attempt to build their relationships with pupils on frequent use of humour or on an over-friendly approach, often find that they are less able to establish and exert their authority when required to do so. The ability to establish mutual respect and rapport in the classroom, and to use humour to good effect, and to be able to establish a friendly ethos without being too friendly, involves very sensitive social awareness on the teacher's part. It is somewhat like a chef who uses taste while cooking to decide on the right amount of salt to enhance the flavour of the dish rather than spoil it. Use of humour and friendship in the classroom can be seen as 'flavour enhancers' to add to the generally business-like and task-oriented manner you convey.

Enhancing pupils' self-esteem

Perhaps the single most important feature that has contributed to improving the quality of education provided in schools has been the increasing awareness amongst teachers of the importance of fostering pupils' self-esteem, self-confidence and self-respect as learners. Many writers have documented the ways in which schools can damage pupils' self-esteem by emphasising for many pupils their relative lack of success compared with that of high-attaining pupils. As a result, such pupils attribute a sense of failure to the work they do, even if it is their best. In consequence, they may then get caught up in a vicious downward spiral of underachievement on their part and low expectations by teachers for their future work. Hargreaves (1982) famously referred to this process as involving the destruction of pupils' sense of dignity, in which they increasingly feel inferior, unable and powerless. He argues that this attack on their dignity stems not only from their experience of the 'formal curriculum', but also, and even more so, from their experience of the 'hidden curriculum'.

The formal curriculum refers to learning about the subject and topic being studied, whereas the hidden curriculum refers to all the messages conveyed to pupils by their experiences in school. These messages stem from the way they are treated, and the attitudes and values conveyed to them about their role and worth as individuals and the worth of what they have accomplished. Many of the messages conveyed in the hidden curriculum may be unintended. For example, if during classroom discussion with pupils you never use or elaborate on pupils' contributions, but always judge them simply in terms of whether they have contributed what you wanted in a narrowly conceived view of their correctness, pupils may get the message that their thoughts and ideas are of little worth or value except in so far as they are correct as judged by you. This may undermine the degree to which they are then willing to contribute ideas, particularly exploratory or uncertain ones, which may be the opposite of what you would wish.

The humanistic approach to teaching and learning

The increasing awareness of the importance of fostering pupils' self-esteem has been a major development over the years. It stems in part from its emphasis within humanistic psychology and its applications to education, notably through the work of Maslow and Rogers (e.g. Maslow, 1987; Rogers and Freiberg, 1994). They both argued that education must place an emphasis on the whole person, on the idea of personal growth, on the pupil's own perspective in terms of how they see themselves and see the world, and on the notions of personal agency and the power of choice. The key elements in applying such an approach to classroom teaching involve:

- seeing the teacher's role as essentially that of a facilitator
- providing pupils with a significant degree of choice and control to manage and organise their learning
- displaying respect for and empathy with pupils.

Studies of the attitudes held by student teachers towards teaching and learning in schools typically show that student teachers tend to hold views consistent with the humanistic approach at the start of their initial training courses, but that by the end of their training they often report that such views are sometimes quite hard to sustain in their actual classroom practice, given the constraints they face in the realities of classroom life (Kyriacou and Cheng, 1993). Nevertheless, despite such difficulties, the classroom climate in schools has become much more humanistic in tone over the years.

Fostering pupils' self-esteem is seen to lie at the heart of this approach. This perspective is evident, either explicitly or implicitly, in many important developments in classroom practice; in particular, the growth of active learning methods, as well as the introduction of new forms of assessment, most notably that of records of achievement. Indeed, some lessons, such as those forming part of a personal and social education programme, are often designed specifically to help foster pupils' self-esteem in general, as well as their self-esteem as learners in particular.

Conveying positive messages

The need to foster pupils' self-esteem as learners is fundamental to establishing a positive classroom climate, and the most important influence on pupils' self-esteem in the classroom is your interaction with the pupils. If your comments to pupils are largely positive, supportive, encouraging, praising, valuing and relaxing, rather than negative, deprecating, harsh, attacking, dominating and anxiety-provoking, this will do much to foster pupils' self-esteem.

In addition, your body language communicates to pupils how you feel about them, through messages conveyed non-verbally by your use of eye contact, posture and facial expression. It can sometimes make it difficult to convey a message verbally about how you feel if your body language indicates to pupils something different. An awareness of how what you say and how your body language is likely to be perceived by pupils can help you to develop the skills involved in establishing a positive classroom climate. Nevertheless, positive messages are much easier to convey if you genuinely do feel in the ways you are trying to convey; that is to say, you genuinely do like and respect pupils, care for their learning, and feel relaxed and confident in your role.

Giving positive help

In your interactions with pupils, the two areas that probably have the greatest effect are how you treat pupils' errors and the extent to which you take a personal interest in their progress.

A pupil error is any contribution that falls short of the standard of progress you desire. It includes a poor answer to a question, a poorly written-up project, or simply not being able to undertake a task you have set. In such circumstances you need to consider the type of feedback to give that will be helpful and supportive rather than admonishing. It is generally better to give specific help that relates to the task rather than critical feedback about performance or critical comments about the pupil. For example, pointing out that the pupil needs to remember that the hypotenuse is always the side opposite to the right angle, is better than simply saying 'You can do better than this' or, even worse, 'This is the low standard of work I have come to expect from you'.

Also, when a pupil is having difficulties, you need to avoid sounding patronising. This can be difficult, because you are in authority and may, from time to time, be giving advice or diagnosing a difficulty that the pupil is already aware of. This should not be a problem, since the pupil should be willing to tolerate it if it only happens occasionally. The real problem arises if your tone is perceived by the pupil to be conveying an element of 'put-down', sarcasm or unfair criticism. Thus, for example, telling a pupil whose diagram would have been much better if a sharpened pencil had been used that 'You should use a pencil sharpener because they're handy for sharpening pencils' would be considered unnecessarily hostile.

You can convey a personal interest in each pupil's progress by relating what you say to each pupil, and how you respond to their progress, to their particular needs and previous work. Learning and using pupils' names with a new class as soon as possible is well worthwhile, and you should certainly know their names after the first few weeks. During personal interactions, indicating to pupils how they are making progress and linking your comments to previous interactions does much to convey to each pupil that you are taking a personal interest in them as individuals and, so far as possible, tailoring matters to meet their individual needs.

Classroom appearance and composition

There are two important features of a lesson that have a major influence on the classroom climate that develops, although neither is part of the lesson itself. The first is the general appearance of the classroom, including its layout and even the appearance of the teacher and that of the pupils. The second is the composition of the class, whether setted, mixed ability or mixed age in composition. Both these features convey strong messages through the hidden curriculum referred to earlier.

Classroom appearance

The general appearance of a classroom indicates to pupils the care that goes into providing them with an environment which is conducive to learning. A clean and well-kept room, with appropriate resources in evidence, which appears comfortable, light and well aired, helps to establish a positive expectation towards the lesson. A positive mental set is also provided by appropriate use of posters and other visual displays relating to the type of work done in the classroom. Displays of pupils' work also indicate a pride in the work achieved, as well as acting as a motivation for those producing display work. Everywhere a pupil looks should convey positive expectations. The degree of light, space and air in the classroom of many schools built since the 1980s has been generally very good. The continued use of temporary huts that have fallen into disrepair, however, requires attention.

While the ethos in the classroom will, in part, be influenced by that of the school in general, each teacher can do much to improve the appearance of their own room, should you – as most teachers do – have your own room. If you are a subject specialist in a secondary school, your room should act as an invitation to the subject. For example, entering a foreign-language classroom should immerse pupils in signals of the foreign countries, most notably through the use of posters, maps and even objects from those countries. While primary school classrooms will be host to a variety of activities, it is often possible to create areas that are subject-specific, and which can also act as a resource area or as a focal point for particular activities.

Layout

The layout of the room should be functional for the purposes intended. At the very least, you and the board should be clearly visible. There is much debate concerning the importance of using a layout to match the general style of teaching and learning that takes place. In 'open classrooms', characterised by more active learning methods, including frequent use of group work, movement of pupils between areas, the use of resource centres, independent work using ICT, the seating arrangements almost certainly requiring desks to be grouped together, and the use of activity-specific areas. In 'traditional classrooms', which emphasise didactic teaching, formal rows of desks are more appropriate.

Unfortunately, the large number of pupils in some classes compared with the physical size of the room itself, often places severe constraints on teachers in creating the most functionally efficient layout. Fortunately, many modern primary schools were designed with open classrooms in mind. This has allowed functionally efficient layouts to be developed, some even making use of movable walls. Secondary schools have generally been much less flexible in this respect. Some schools have developed well laid-out resource centres housed in rooms of their own, where teachers can send a pupil or groups of pupils to undertake particular tasks, either unsupervised or supervised by a teacher based in the resource centre.

Tidiness

It is also very important to keep the classroom clean and tidy. This can have a marked impact on pupils when they first arrive at the classroom, whether it be at the beginning of the school day or after a break. In primary schools one can make efforts to ensure that pupils themselves help to keep things tidy and avoid making a mess. This tends to be more difficult in secondary schools, where you will be teaching many different classes, and may not always be using your own room. If on occasion you take over a room where desks and tables have been left disarranged, it is well worthwhile to tidy up quickly before your class arrives. You, of course, also have a responsibility to colleagues to ensure that any room you leave is fit and ready for the next user, which includes cleaning the blackboard. This is all part of having a professional attitude towards your work.

Dress

Your appearance conveys messages to pupils about the care and attention you give to presentation in general. It is the case that in our society, dress conveys signals about status and about your formal role. However, the norms that operate here are changing all the time. For example, in some schools, school uniform is worn by pupils, female teachers are expected not to wear trousers, most male teachers wear a jacket and tie, teachers may be addressed as 'Sir' or 'Miss' and pupils are addressed by their surnames. At the other extreme, there are schools where none of these apply. Whatever else, you will need to adapt to the conventions and expectations that operate in your school, as radical deviations away from these are likely to be misunderstood by pupils, although some degree of departure in the direction you feel is educationally worthwhile is acceptable and desirable. Nevertheless, your behaviour in the classroom must take account of your role in also contributing to a consistent and coherent attempt by staff in the school as a whole to operate as a team in developing and emphasising certain values and expectations.

While you will have little control over pupils' dress, other than dealing with major departures from school conventions (such as wearing earrings or jeans), it is important to insist they arrive at the lesson prepared for the tasks to be undertaken, with appropriate

Your appearance will convey a message about you

equipment, such as pens, pencils and rulers. Bags should not be left on desks and coats should not be worn. In some schools, dealing with such apparently minor matters can involve a lot of time and effort on the part of teachers. In such cases, well-developed routines are of immense value in helping to ensure a prompt start to the lesson.

Class composition

The pupil composition of the class also conveys important messages. A class composed of pupils setted or streamed in terms of attainment will almost certainly have an influence on pupils' expectations about themselves and on your expectations about them. It is particularly important to ensure that those groups identified as average or below average in attainment are not discouraged and do not underachieve as a result.

Mixed-ability groups are often used to convey a sense that all pupils are equally valued, which in part explains their widespread adoption in comprehensive schools and in primary schools, although in the latter it is often simply the most convenient form of group given the size of the year group. In some primary schools and for some secondary school (morning registration) tutor groups, cross-age groups are used, and these may be composed of quite a wide age range. Other aspects of pupil composition of importance include social class mix, ethnic origin mix, and the proportion of able pupils or pupils with learning difficulties.

All such factors have an important bearing on teaching and learning. They also have an important bearing on the type of classroom climate that develops, and on the ways you can best facilitate a positive classroom culture. The key factor here is the skill involved in developing mutual respect and rapport that takes the composition of the class into account. Establishing your authority, being sociable and motivating pupils will require different shared understandings and points of reference with classes that may be composed very differently.

Thus, for example, the way in which pupils in general may react to your use of humour, how supportive your feedback needs to be, the way you exert discipline, and how you try to personalise interactions, may well be quite different for a group of racially mixed pupils in an infant class in a school serving a relatively deprived urban catchment, compared with a group of top-set pupils at a sixth form college serving a prosperous rural catchment. An important aspect of your skill in establishing a positive classroom climate is your sensitivity to the effect of your behaviour on the type of pupils that make up the class and the context within which this occurs.

Further reading

Brophy, J. E. (2004) *Motivating Students to Learn*, 2nd edn. New York: Lawrence Erlbaum. A very readable overview of the ways in which teachers can use a variety of strategies in order to foster and sustain pupil motivation in the classroom.

Campbell, J., Kyriakides, L., Muijs, D. and Robinson, W. (2004) *Assessing Teacher Effectiveness: Developing a Differentiated Model*. London: RoutledgeFalmer. This book identifies the values held by teachers regarding teaching and learning and how these values affect the type of classroom climate they seek to establish.

Cullingford, C. (2003) *The Best Years of their Lives? Pupils' Experiences of School*. London: RoutledgeFalmer. This book is based on interviews with pupils and explores their views about their experience of schooling and the effect of the classroom climate on their learning.

Watkins, C. (2005) *Classrooms as Learning Communities: What's in it for Schools?* London: RoutledgeFalmer. A readable overview of the teaching skills involved in eliciting and sustaining a high level of pupil engagement and a sense of belonging.

Key questions about your classroom climate

1 Is the classroom climate purposeful, task-oriented, relaxed, warm and supportive, and does it have a sense of order?
2 Do my comments, particularly feedback on their progress, help pupils to develop self-esteem and self-respect as learners?
3 Are the learning activities challenging and do they offer realistic opportunities for success?
4 Do I make good use of both intrinsic and extrinsic sources of pupil motivation?
5 Does my behaviour convey positive expectations?
6 Do I successfully convey a personal interest and care for the progress of each pupil?
7 Is my relationship with pupils based on mutual respect and rapport?
8 Do the messages conveyed by the nature and types of activities used and the way I interact with pupils contribute to establishing a positive classroom climate?
9 Does the appearance and layout of the classroom convey positive expectations and facilitate the activities which occur?
10 Do I take account of the influence of the composition of the class (e.g. spread of ability, social class mix) on the way I can best establish a positive classroom climate?

6 Discipline

Discipline refers to the order that is necessary in the classroom for pupil learning to occur effectively. There is a massive amount of literature on discipline in schools, which includes a number of books offering sound practical advice (Chaplain, 2003; Porter, 2000; Rogers, 2006), those reporting the results of research studies dealing with the views and experiences of pupils and teachers, including student teachers (e.g. Evertson and Weinstein, 2006; Kyriacou *et al.,* 2007), and major government reports on the topic, such as the Steer Report (Steer, 2005). Discipline is one of the main areas of concern for student teachers, and is also widely identified as a major area of need within the in-service education of experienced teachers.

Developing the skills needed to establish discipline in the classroom is one of the major challenges facing beginning teachers and, not surprisingly, features in the TDA (2007) QTS standards. The TDA refers to discipline in terms of establishing a clear framework to manage pupils' behaviour constructively and to promote pupils' self-control and independence, and requires student teachers to be able to use a range of behaviour management strategies.

Clearly, order is needed in the classroom if the activities that take place are to facilitate effective learning by pupils. The most important point to bear in mind in considering discipline is that creating the necessary order is more to do with the skills involved in effective teaching in general than it is to do with how you deal with pupil misbehaviour itself. If the learning activities are well planned and prepared, if the presentation elicits and maintains pupils' attention, interest and involvement, and if the activities are challenging and offer realistic opportunities for success, then the necessary order will be established as part of these qualities. In essence, skilful teaching as outlined in the previous chapters lies at the heart of establishing discipline.

Nevertheless, pupil misbehaviour will occur from time to time, even in the lessons of the most skilful teachers, and has to be dealt with. However, it is a mistake to view discipline as something concerned with how you deal with pupil misbehaviour, separate from your general teaching. It is an even worse mistake to try to establish discipline by focusing on how to dominate and engender fear in pupils as a strategy for minimising misbehaviour. Such a course of action is undesirable, not only because it will undermine your efforts to create the positive classroom climate necessary to facilitate pupils learning effectively, but also because it directs your attention away from considering how to develop the quality of your teaching as the primary means of establishing order.

The nature of pupil misbehaviour

Most pupil misbehaviour is quite trivial. The types of pupil misbehaviour most frequently cited by teachers are:

- excessive talk or talking out of turn
- being noisy (both verbal, such as shouting to another pupil across the room, and non-verbal, such as dropping bags onto the floor)

- not paying attention to the teacher
- not getting on with the work required
- being out of their seat without good cause
- hindering other pupils
- arriving late for lessons.

To a large extent, such problems can be minimised by skilful teaching in general, and by developing conventions and routines for behaviour that are followed. More serious types of misbehaviour (verbal aggression to another pupil, bad language and cheek, disobedience, refusal to accept authority, and physical destructiveness) are much less frequent and are likely to occur if the lesser forms of pupil misbehaviour are allowed to become commonplace, or if pupils are reacting against personal and academic difficulties they are facing.

In thinking about pupil misbehaviour, we need to remember that there is a continuum of such behaviour ranging from quite trivial acts to very serious ones. Moreover, the standard of behaviour expected will vary from teacher to teacher. One teacher may insist on virtual silence in a lesson while pupils are working, whereas another might be happy with a marked degree of background talking. In addition, pupils will also vary in their attitudes towards good behaviour. Some pupils will be happy to wait quietly while a teacher looks for some equipment in a storeroom, whereas some pupils will be poised to take any such opportunity to engage in rowdy behaviour. The discipline that prevails in your classroom will not only be influenced by your behaviour and expectations, but also by the expectations pupils bring with them and, importantly, by the prevailing ethos in the school. Nevertheless, a well-managed lesson coupled with a relationship based on mutual respect and rapport will do much to minimise pupil misbehaviour. Indeed, even in schools where it is recognised that there are a number of pupils with marked emotional or academic difficulties, skilful teaching can ensure that good discipline in lessons will be the norm.

Causes of pupil misbehaviour

In general, you can start with the assumption that all pupils will be willing to engage in the work, and are only likely to misbehave if there are specific reasons or motives for doing so. As such, your task is to make it as easy as possible for pupils to sustain good behaviour. The main causes of misbehaviour in the classroom are as follows:

- *Boredom.* If the activities are presented in a manner that fails to elicit and sustain their interest, or if the activity lasts for too long and fails to be stimulating, or if the activity is too easy or is felt to lack relevance, then pupils are likely to become bored.
- *Prolonged mental effort.* Most academic work requires sustained mental effort, and this is demanding. Everyone finds that sustaining mental effort for long periods is difficult and, at times, unpleasant.
- *Inability to do the work.* Pupils may be unable to do the work set, either because it is too difficult or because they are unclear about the task demands.
- *Being sociable.* Pupils have a complex social life in schools, in which friendships are made, conflicts arise and interests are shared. Aspects of these social relationships

between pupils will often spill over into a lesson (e.g. pupils may resume a conversation started during the break period).

- *Low academic self-esteem.* Some pupils will lack confidence in themselves as learners, and may have experienced frequent failure in the past that makes them reluctant to engage in academic tasks for fear of further failure (failing because you did not try is much less painful than failing if you did). Such pupils can become quite alienated from the academic expectations that form part of a positive classroom climate.

- *Emotional difficulties.* Some pupils may have emotional problems which make it difficult for them to adjust to and cope with the demands of school life and the academic demands of the classroom. It may be because they are being bullied in school, or because they are neglected at home. In many cases, such pupils may become attention seeking, and actually enjoy the attention they provoke from you or their fellow pupils for misbehaving.

- *Poor attitudes.* Some pupils may simply not value doing well at school and, to the extent that problems arise, such as finding the work boring or difficult, will switch off their effort. Moreover, some may try to avoid doing the work by arriving late to lessons, or keeping a low profile while doing little. When challenged, they may be apologetic or hostile, but still do little. Some pupils may deliberately make a nuisance of themselves simply to cause excitement.

- *Lack of negative consequences.* Whenever a pupil misbehaves, your actions that follow in consequence must be aimed at getting the pupil involved in the work again as quickly as possible. Furthermore, your behaviour should act to dissuade such pupil misbehaviour occurring again in similar circumstances. If pupil misbehaviour is not picked up quickly and discouraged by the consequences that follow, it is likely to become more frequent.

Implications for teaching

It will be evident from looking at these main causes of pupil misbehaviour that they have different implications for how you can best deal with such incidents. For example, if a pupil fails to pay attention because they are finding the topic boring, your best course of action will be quite different than if the problem stems from worries and anxieties the pupil has because the work seems too difficult. Part of the skill of teaching involves being sensitive to the different causes of pupil misbehaviour. While most of the time sound management techniques and the most obvious assumptions about the cause of the misbehaviour are appropriate, skilful teachers are alert to circumstances where an exploratory probe in private is needed. This will be evident if a pupil's behaviour appears to be out of character or if the normal management techniques do not appear to be having their expected effect. Skilful teachers are also very adept at picking up subtle cues from a pupil's facial expression or tone of voice that might indicate an underlying cause for concern.

An important point to bear in mind about the causes of misbehaviour is that pupils are a captive audience. Unlike many activities in life, where we have some degree of choice over whether we participate and can often withdraw from a situation that we find unpleasant, pupils are required to attend lessons. Moreover, they are not allowed to opt out of learning. In all teaching there is therefore an implicit tension underlying the activities, namely that if pupils do not engage freely in the activities set up by the teacher, they will be coerced to do so. Poor progress is not simply the concern of the pupil, but also the concern of the teacher and the pupil's parents. Most people will find, from time to time, that being trapped in a situation that is unpleasant and from which they cannot escape is extremely frustrating. If they are also coerced to participate, the sense of frustration can become unbearable. The most serious incidents of pupil misbehaviour are likely to occur when such a tension has built up, and when the pupil feels your attention is aggressive and coercive rather than sympathetic and supportive. A warning signal of this might be the pupil looking increasingly angry or tense, and perhaps claiming to be picked upon or treated unfairly in some way. The skills involved in being sensitive to whether a pupil is feeling tense in this way, and the ability to defuse such a feeling, are very important in preventing serious incidents occurring.

Establishing your authority

The key to establishing good discipline in the classroom lies in pupils accepting your authority to manage their behaviour and their progress in learning. Learning activities cannot take place effectively in a classroom full of 30 pupils unless you are given authority to control, manage and direct what is going on, as and when appropriate. All pupils recognise this from their earliest days in school, but it is important to note that this authority is given to you to act as a manager of their learning rather than as a power relationship. A useful analogy is with the authority you give to a tour guide to show you around places of interest in a particular city. You obey instructions about where and when to go to different places and what to do there because you trust and expect that in doing so you will get to see what is worth seeing efficiently. Your trust largely rests on the expertise and skill you expect your tour guide to have. Similarly, establishing your authority as a teacher largely depends on four main aspects of your role:

- conveying your status
- teaching competently
- exercising managerial control
- dealing with pupil misbehaviour effectively.

Conveying your status

Much of your authority as a teacher derives from the status you have in that role, and the respect and esteem for teachers generally held in society; this is particularly conveyed to pupils by their parents and other sources of influence. You are also an adult, and will have some degree of status because of this, most notably with younger pupils where you may be perceived as a parent figure to some extent. If you have a formal post of seniority in the school, such as being the headteacher or the deputy head, then this will also add to your status.

The most important thing about status, however, is not that you simply have such status, but that you act as though you have status. This conveys to pupils a sense of you being in charge and in authority that they simply take for granted. Behaving as though you have status will be conveyed by your appearing relaxed, self-assured and confident, as indicated in particular by your tone of voice, posture, facial expression and use of eye contact. When you issue an instruction, your tone will indicate by its matter-of-factness that you simply expect without question that the instruction will be followed.

Status is also conveyed by various actions that indicate you have status: for example, you are free to wander around the classroom, initiate conversations and direct activities. You also take the decisions about when pupils are to start and stop particular activities. Again, it is by acting in these ways, in a manner that indicates that you are in charge, that you create a climate in which your authority is taken for granted. This requires that as well as behaving in these ways yourself, you control such behaviour by pupils; i.e. pupils cannot wander about, decide when to stop activities, or when to initiate conversations with you or with each other unless it is with your permission and is appropriate. Thus, for example, most teachers will make a point of picking up on pupils who have started to pack away their books near the end of a lesson before they have been told to do so.

It is perhaps worth noting that one aspect of conveying status you need to be careful about is the use of touch. It is quite common for those in a position of higher status to touch those of lower status, in a friendly and caring manner, but not vice versa. However, you do need to be aware that in the classroom, touching pupils in this way can be misunderstood and, in part depending on the pupil's personal circumstances, even undesirable or unpleasant; touching pupils should be avoided.

Conveying your status

Teaching competently

The second major source of your authority comes from teaching competently. If you convey to pupils that you are knowledgeable about the topic or subject, are interested in it, and can set up the learning activities skilfully, then pupils will respect your ability to teach; this will confirm your authority to manage their behaviour. This requires that your lessons are well planned and prepared, that your manner conveys interest and enthusiasm, and that you can set up challenging activities effectively.

One of the reasons that teaching competently is so crucial to establishing your authority, is that poor teaching is often experienced as insulting. When pupils are taught in a way they regard as unsatisfactory, they commonly make one of two interpretations: either the teacher has not made an effort, which implies that the pupils are not worth making an effort for; or the school has allocated them a teacher who lacks adequate teaching skills, which implies that the pupils were not worth being allocated a better teacher. Both interpretations strike at the heart of pupils' self-esteem, and the extent to which they react by misbehaviour is largely related to the underlying insult they experience. In contrast, being taught competently engenders a feeling of pride and self-respect, and affirms their sense of worth and importance.

Exercising managerial control

The third major source of your authority comes from exercising managerial control in the classroom. In order to set up learning activities efficiently, lessons need to get off to a prompt start, pupils must be kept involved in the learning activities, and transitions between activities should be handled smoothly. Anything that frustrates these will require you to exert managerial control. Pupils arriving late for lessons, not paying attention or applying sufficient effort, or interrupting your presentation, can frustrate the prompt start and flow of the lesson. Smith and Laslett (1992) famously identified the four main tasks of classroom management as 'Get them in, get them out, get on with it, and get on with them!'

The most crucial aspects of exercising managerial control involve establishing clear conventions, routines and expectations for pupils' behaviour, and imposing your view on a situation when any conflicts arise. For example, if when you are ready to start the lesson and have called the pupils to attention, a pupil points out that they need a new exercise book, rather than allow the start of the lesson to be delayed, you should indicate that you will deal with that later and proceed promptly with the lesson. Once the lesson has started, virtually any activity can frustrate the progress of the lesson. For example, giving out equipment can take too long or become cumbersome, the pace of work by pupils may be rather slow, or pupils may take a long time to pay attention to you after an activity has been completed. To prevent the progress being frustrated, you need to exercise your control whenever appropriate.

In order to exercise managerial control, pupils' behaviour needs to be rule-governed. Indeed, a study by Kyriacou *et al.* (2007), exploring the views of beginning teachers in six counties on strategies they thought were effective in dealing with pupil misbehaviour in the classroom, found that the strategy they viewed as most effective was 'establishing clear and consistent school and classroom rules about the behaviours that are acceptable and that are unacceptable'. In contrast, strategies such as issuing reprimands and punishments were regarded as much less effective. In general, the beginning teachers saw a combination of establishing sound classroom rules and counselling pupils towards re-engaging with their work with the minimum amount of fuss, as being the most effective approach to dealing with pupil misbehaviour.

Such classroom rules may be explicitly stated by teachers or simply inferred from the teacher's actions. In a study of secondary school teachers, Wragg (2005) identified 11 classroom rules that were explicitly stated by teachers or could be clearly inferred from their actions. These were (in order of occurrence):

- There must be no talking when the teacher is talking.
- There must be no disruptive noises.
- Rules for entering, leaving and moving in classrooms.
- There must be no interference with the work of others.
- Work must be completed in a specified way.
- Pupils must raise hand to answer, not shout out.
- Pupils must make a positive effort in their work.
- Pupils must not challenge the authority of the teacher.
- Respect must be shown for property and equipment.
- Rules to do with safety.
- Pupils must ask if they do not understand.

In looking at primary school teachers, Wragg (2005) identified a similar set of rules in operation. However, he noted that the primary school teachers' initial encounters with their new classes were generally characterised by a friendly smile, business-like manner and benign firmness, whereas the secondary school teachers had been more aggressively assertive.

Unpredictable events, such as the appearance of a window cleaner, can be disruptive, although a quick acknowledgement of the situation with a touch of humour is often effective in such circumstances. Imposing your will simply means ensuring that pupils do what you want them to do to ensure that the lesson progresses.

Dealing with pupil misbehaviour effectively

From time to time, pupil misbehaviour will occur. This may range from a trivial incident, such as a pupil not paying attention, to a serious one, such as a pupil punching another in anger. How you deal with pupil misbehaviour is the fourth major source of your authority. Your authority will be enhanced to the extent that you are able to deal with pupil misbehaviour effectively and fairly. How to do this is the subject of the remainder of this chapter. However, it is important to bear in mind that the type of strategy that will work best not only depends on the teacher's skilful use of these strategies, but also their ability to take account of the context in which they are working and in which the misbehaviour occurs.

The approach to dealing with disruptive behaviour advocated by Rogers (1998, 2006) highlights the importance of having a well-thought-out repertoire of techniques that can be brought into play in a skilful manner, so that pupils can be guided towards re-engaging with the work as quickly as possible and be given a clear idea of what is regarded by the teacher as unacceptable behaviour.

Pre-empting pupil misbehaviour

In considering pupil misbehaviour, 'prevention is better than cure'. Skilful teaching can do much to minimise pupil misbehaviour occurring in the first place, and can usefully re-direct incidents that were developing before they need be regarded as misbehaviour. The essence of pre-empting misbehaviour lies in vigilance plus action.

Strategies to pre-empt misbehaviour

Careful monitoring of pupils' behaviour and progress during a lesson can ensure that most misbehaviour is nipped in the bud. Successful monitoring requires a conscious decision to do so periodically, as it is all too easy to get wrapped up in particular activities, such as giving individual help, and thereby not to notice another pupil who is disrupting someone else's work. Experienced teachers are adept at such monitoring, while student teachers can usefully remind themselves to do this until it becomes routine.

The main useful strategies to pre-empt misbehaviour are as follows.

- *Scan the classroom.* Periodically look around the classroom and consider whether any pupils appear to be having difficulties and, if so, go over and investigate in a supportive and helpful manner to ensure that pupils resume working as quickly as possible. Individual contact will be more effective than shouting across the room. The latter both disrupts other pupils unnecessarily and tends to assume the pupil is misbehaving.
- *Circulate.* Circulate around the room periodically and probe whether pupils are having difficulties. Sometimes asking a pupil about their progress usefully uncovers problems that they would otherwise not have drawn to your attention.
- *Make eye contact.* When addressing the class as a whole, make eye contact with individual pupils periodically, but do not look too long at any individual. If you suspect a pupil may be misbehaving, making eye contact, and prolonging it, will indicate to that pupil your awareness of their need to re-involve themselves in the lesson without needing to signal this publicly or interrupt the flow of the lesson.
- *Target your questions.* Directing your questions around the class helps to maintain pupils' involvement; targeting questions at particular individuals is also a signal to them to get re-involved.
- *Use proximity.* While you normally stand at the front of the classroom, how and where you move to can be an effective signal of your monitoring. By moving towards two pupils talking, you can indicate your awareness to them of this without interrupting the lesson. You may also stand near a pair or group of pupils for some time to sustain their working.

- *Give academic help.* Giving advice and guidance to pupils to enable and encourage them to make progress with the task in hand is the single most powerful means of pre-empting misbehaviour.

- *Change activities or pace.* As a result of monitoring pupils' progress you may feel the lesson is proceeding too slowly or too fast and that pupils are ready to move on to another activity or are running into difficulties. Your decisions about altering the pace of the lesson and when to change the activity are crucial to maintaining pupils' involvement. This applies not only to the class as a whole, but also to individual pupils, some of whom may need to work at a different pace or on a different activity, even when whole-class teaching is taking place, if they are to sustain their involvement to best effect.

- *Notice misbehaviour.* If a pupil is misbehaving, in the vast majority of cases it is important to indicate to the pupil that you have noticed this. Eye contact may be sufficient, or if you wish to be more forceful, a stern facial expression or a pause in your exposition will indicate your concern and displeasure, while not interrupting the flow of the lesson for more than a moment. Student teachers often tend to refrain from doing this, in part because they feel misbehaviour needs to be more formally reprimanded once it is noticed or because they hope it might disappear if ignored. In fact, signalling of this sort is very important and effective in exercising managerial control; failing to do so by ignoring simply allows more frequent or serious misbehaviour to develop, whereas too ready a recourse to reprimands serves to create a conflict unnecessarily.

- *Notice disrespect.* When interacting with pupils you should expect them to behave with appropriate respect. Thus, for example, if a pupil is slouched in their seat when addressed by you, it would be a normal courtesy for the pupil to quickly sit up straight while replying. If they do not do so, you might deal with it by looking surprised or stern to indicate you are not happy with this, and if that is not sufficient you might comment explicitly. Lack of courtesy or respect towards you needs to be picked up as it forms part of pupils' impressions about the standard of behaviour you expect and the type of relationship you wish to establish. Not doing so will tacitly undermine your authority in behaving with status and exercising managerial control on your terms.

- *Move pupils.* If the circumstances warrant, do not hesitate to separate two pupils who are not behaving acceptably together, after due warning to this effect. Alternatively, you may require a particular pupil to sit at the front where you can monitor the pupil's behaviour more closely. Seating arrangements are a privilege rather than a right of pupils, and if you feel a better arrangement is desirable, a move can be helpful. However, you need to emphasise that this is done in the pupils' interests, to ensure that any resentment is minimised.

Sound discipline largely rests on skilful teaching and skilful use of such strategies to pre-empt misbehaviour. Even so, misbehaviour will still occur from time to time, and to deal with this the best strategy is to combine the use of investigating and counselling with the use of reprimands.

Investigating and counselling

When pupil misbehaviour has occurred despite your use of pre-emptive strategies, you have a choice to make between investigating the nature and cause of the misbehaviour or reprimanding the misbehaviour on the basis of your reading of its most likely nature and cause. Your decision will very much depend on the context, such as the pupil concerned, the nature of the activities taking place, how certain you are about your reading of the incident, and what you anticipate will be the most likely effect of any action you take.

Investigating and counselling is a strategy whereby you approach the incident of mis-behaviour with a view to finding out the nature of the problem. Indeed, your comment to the pupil might well be 'What's the problem?' Your tone should indicate your concern with a view to helping the pupil return to the work in hand as soon as possible, rather than convey hostility or aggression on your part. In such circumstances, the pupil may admit to having problems with their work, or may attribute the misbehaviour to being bored, being provoked by another pupil, or whatever. If the nature of the problem is not primarily an academic difficulty, you then need to decide whether to counsel the pupil towards behaving appropriately there and then or else seeing the pupil at the end of the lesson, during a break time or after school.

Effective counselling

When counselling a pupil it is important to allow the pupil to do much of the talking, with a view to helping them to see that the misbehaviour is not in their interests, and that the pupil should agree to behave as required in future. Such counselling is likely to be more effective if conducted in private, in a context of trust and mutual respect, and where you convey a caring and concerned attitude. It is important to the pupils to evaluate their own behaviour and to consider the consequences, such as poor academic progress or punishment, that may follow if the behaviour does not improve. The most important aspect of counselling is to end with the pupil agreeing to behave well in future as a positive decision.

Where such counselling does not appear to be successful or serious problems appear to be underlying the misbehaviour, it is important to confer with colleagues who have explicit pastoral care concerns. In secondary schools, this will be the form teacher and the head of house or year, although in many secondary schools it is usual for the head of department to be involved in the first instance. In primary schools, the class teacher is normally the form teacher as well, and thus consultation is likely to involve the headteacher or a deputy head with specific responsibility for pastoral care.

Your pastoral care role

In your role as a class teacher, you must bear in mind that you simultaneously have a pastoral care role. Hence, as well as being concerned about pupils' academic progress, you must also be concerned about their general behaviour and attitudes, their personal and social development, and any individual needs they may have. Dealing with pupil mis-behaviour is not simply a matter of discipline, but is also bound up with your pastoral care responsibilities.

In addition, in this respect you should also be alert to pupils' behaviour giving cause for concern that may not undermine discipline or be regarded as misbehaviour. For example, excessive shyness, a tendency to work very slowly, or frequent day-dreaming, may not be in any way disruptive, but may well need to be picked up in monitoring pupils' progress and may well need to be investigated further. Indeed, picking up on non-disruptive behaviours such as inattentiveness or an unwillingness to participate in activities can sometimes be a sign of personal problems in the pupil's life (such as being bullied, or worries about a parent who is seriously ill) and identifying this can enable the teacher and school to offer the pupil appropriate help and support (Kyriacou, 2003).

Such concerns are linked to the Every Child Matters agenda, and this is recognised by inclusion in the TDA (2007) QTS standards of the need for student teachers to be aware of the legal requirements, national policies and guidance on the safeguarding and promotion of pupils' well-being.

Resulting actions

As a result of investigating and counselling by you alone or in wider consultation with colleagues, there may well be actions you need to take to assist the pupil to behave well. For example, you may discover that the pupil finds it difficult to settle down to work because they are easily distracted by certain other pupils, or the pupil is finding the work too difficult or is getting late nights at home. Some pupils may have a special educational need that requires a formal assessment to be made and explicit provision, such as the help of a support teacher for a period. Some of the necessary actions can be taken by you in the classroom; others may involve collaboration with colleagues, particularly if parents and other agencies are to be involved.

Using reprimands

A reprimand refers to an explicit verbal warning or comment by you to a pupil which indicates your disapproval of the misbehaviour that has occurred. Because the use of investigating and counselling is time-consuming and logistically too difficult to be used for every misbehaviour that occurs, most misbehaviour that has not been successfully dealt with by the pre-emptive strategies will be dealt with by reprimands; only a minority of problems are dealt with by recourse to investigating and counselling. However, the balance between these two strategies will vary greatly from lesson to lesson and from class to class.

Effective use of reprimands

Reprimands are best used sparingly and should complement skilful teaching in general. Too frequent a use of reprimands will lessen their effect, will undermine creating a positive classroom climate, and is experienced by some pupils as 'nagging'.

A number of qualities are involved in the skilful and effective use of reprimands.

- *Target correctly.* The pupil being reprimanded should be correctly identified as the pupil instigating or engaged in the misbehaviour. A particular danger here is to reprimand a pupil who was reacting to another's provocation

- *Be firm.* Your reprimand should be clear and firm in tone and content. Avoid pleading or implying damage limitation (e.g. 'Let's at least get some decent work done in the last ten minutes') or softening your reprimand once it has been issued.

- *Express concern.* Your reprimand should convey your concern that the pupil's interests or those of other pupils are being harmed by the misbehaviour.

- *Avoid anger.* While a firm expression of disapproval is effective, expressing intense anger, shouting at pupils, and appearing to have lost your temper will tend to undermine a positive classroom climate. Frequent expressions of anger are undesirable, are experienced by pupils as unpleasant and, with younger pupils in particular, may be very upsetting.

- *Emphasise what is required.* Reprimands should emphasise what pupils should be doing rather than simply complain about the misbehaviour itself. 'Pay attention' is better than 'Stop looking out of the window', while 'You may talk quietly with your neighbour' is better than 'There's too much noise in here'.

- *Maintain psychological impact.* When a reprimand is given, its impact is enhanced by non-verbal cues, such as eye contact. After the reprimand is given, a momentary prolonging of eye contact together with a slight pause before continuing with the lesson can increase the force of the exchange.

- *Avoid confrontations.* Do not force a pupil into a heated exchange. Where such a possibility seems likely because the pupil appears tense, agitated or unresponsive to your pre-emptive strategies, postponing a reprimand and instead using investigating and counselling strategies would be appropriate. If you reprimand a pupil who then reacts emotionally, you can usefully curtail the exchange by telling the pupil to stay behind at the end of the lesson in a matter-of-fact manner and quickly resume the lesson.

- *Criticise the behaviour not the pupil.* It is important to emphasise that you disapprove of the misbehaviour not the pupil. This enables you to convey a sense of caring for the pupil and their interests, and gives pupils an opportunity to dissociate themselves from such misbehaviour in future. 'You need to concentrate more on your work and spend less time chatting to others' is better than 'You're an idle person'.

- *Use private rather than public reprimands.* A private reprimand, such as a quiet word, is useful because it is a more personal contact and lessens the likelihood of embarrassing the pupil and the chance that the pupil might react with hostility. It is also less disruptive to other pupils. A public reprimand to a pupil is better only when there is a specific reason to go public, such as when you actually want the whole class to hear the reprimand as an implicit warning to others. A less disruptive use of a public reprimand is to simply call out the pupil's name in a tone that conveys that you have noticed some misbehaviour which must stop immediately.

- *Be pre-emptive.* Reprimands aimed at pre-empting misbehaviour are more effective than those that follow only after repeated and prolonged misbehaviour.
- *State rules and rationale.* A reprimand can usefully consist of a statement of the rule being transgressed together with an explanation of why the rule is required for the benefit of teaching and learning (e.g. 'Please put up your hand and wait until I ask you to speak so that everyone gets a fair chance to contribute and we can all hear what is said').
- *Avoid making hostile remarks.* Hostile and deprecating remarks should be avoided, as pupils may feel personally disliked, and may become disaffected and alienated. Sarcasm and ridicule in particular are felt by pupils to be unfair, and can undermine mutual respect and rapport to the detriment of a positive classroom climate.
- *Avoid unfair comparisons.* Pupils tend to feel that reprimands which involve stereotyping or comparisons with others are unfair, particularly if they relate to other members of the pupil's family or other classes (e.g. 'Your sister's work is much better than this' or 'Just because this is set three doesn't mean you don't have to pay attention').
- *Be consistent.* Reprimands should relate to clear and consistently applied expectations. Pupils will resent being reprimanded if they feel the behaviour was not the type you would normally reprimand or if the severity of the reprimand was unexpectedly great.
- *Do not make empty threats.* Do not issue reprimands that threaten consequences you would not wish to or could not carry out (e.g. 'The next pupil who talks will go straight to the head' or 'If you make another insolent remark, I shall be contacting your parents'). If you explicitly state consequences that will follow, it is very important to carry these out if you are to maintain credibility when you use this strategy in the future.
- *Avoid reprimanding the whole class.* Reprimanding the whole class is a serious act and should only be used when certain misbehaviour or your cause for concern is so widespread that individual reprimands will not have sufficient effect or be appropriate. In order to avoid casting your criticism equally on all pupils, including the blameless, it is useful to indicate your concern with 'too many pupils' rather than all pupils. A useful alternative is to discuss with the class as a whole why certain misbehaviour has become widespread, so that you can identify any particular problems and reinforce the need for good behaviour.
- *Making an example.* Another useful alternative to reprimanding the whole class is to issue a particularly forceful reprimand to one pupil, adding or implying that you will not tolerate other pupils acting in this way. Reprimanding an individual can have just as much impact on the behaviour of the class as reprimanding the whole class. Making an example can be particularly useful in the first few lessons with a new class to highlight your expectations, such as how you deal with the first pupil who arrives late for your lessons without any excuse. It is also useful if certain pupils appear to be trying to challenge your authority publicly; however, you must be sensitive about whether you are simply being drawn into a public confrontation that is best dealt with in some other way.

Ideally the use of reprimands can be thought of as adding a few drops of oil to an engine that is running well but very occasionally needs further lubrication to maintain its smooth operation. Once the use of reprimands becomes frequent, the climate of the lesson can change quite markedly, and the tone becomes one of the teacher trying to coerce and cajole pupils towards working well. In such circumstances you need to think carefully whether the academic demands made upon pupils can be modified and consider the nature of the underlying causes of such continuing conflict.

Indeed, frequent misbehaviour by pupils acts as an on-going critique by pupils of the demands made upon them, and has acted as a major stimulus for curriculum development. The point being stressed here is that if the skilful use of reprimands does not appear to be successful, you should not assume that the best way ahead is to resort to more frequent and more severe reprimands and the use of punishments or other related strategies without first thinking long and hard about the educational context within which the problem over discipline has arisen.

Using punishments

Despite the skilful use of reprimands and other strategies already discussed, pupil misbehaviour may persist. In such circumstances, the use of punishments may be effective in restoring discipline.

The nature and purpose of punishment

A punishment is in essence a formal action which the pupil is intended to experience as unpleasant, as a means of helping the pupil to behave appropriately in the future. The dividing line between a reprimand and a punishment is often blurred because reprimands and other strategies are often also experienced as unpleasant. The difference largely lies in the formal way in which a punishment is set up and the explicit intention for it to be unpleasant.

In setting up a punishment, you thus need to emphasise to the pupil that the use of punishment is intended to help the pupil appreciate the gravity and seriousness with which you are treating the misbehaviour and the urgency of the need for acceptable behaviour to occur in future. Indeed, it is essential that the pupil sees the punishment as being in their own interests, and certainly not as an expression of malice or hostility.

Punishments have three main purposes:

- *Retribution:* the idea that justice requires that wrongdoing is followed by a morally deserved punishment.
- *Deterrence:* the idea that the pupil or other pupils will wish to avoid such misbehaviour in the future for fear of the consequences.
- *Rehabilitation:* the idea that the pupil will be helped to understand the moral wrongdoing of the misbehaviour and the need to behave well in future.

In schools, punishments often involve all three purposes to some extent, but rehabilitation is clearly the most important one and the one that embodies an educational purpose to enable a pupil to choose to behave well in the future. Deterrence is also important and may contribute to the effectiveness of your expressions of disapproval when using reprimands. Retribution tends to be the most evident when a moral code has been broken: an action which the teacher feels needs to be punished in the interests of justice as an expression of the school community's disapproval, the most notable examples being bullying, stealing, cheating, vandalism and certain types of verbal abuse.

The shortcomings of punishment

The most important aspect of punishment to bear in mind is that its impact is largely dependent on it being used as a formal and weighty sanction employed for serious incidents of misbehaviour when other strategies have been unsuccessful. There is, however, an element of illusion involved here, since very few sanctions are in fact of any weight, with most involving only a short period of unpleasantness or having a nuisance value. Their impact owes much more to using them in a way that conveys the seriousness with which the misbehaviour is being viewed. It is also largely the case that the type of pupils most likely to be punished, notably disaffected pupils who have little respect for authority and the values and ethos of the school, are the pupils least likely to respond by better behaviour in future. In contrast, those pupils who would be most worried about punishment are those pupils for whom skilful use of other strategies should be sufficiently effective.

The main drawbacks of using punishments are:

- They form an inappropriate model for human relationships.
- They foster anxiety and resentment.
- They have a short-lived 'initial shock' effect.
- They encourage pupils to develop strategies to avoid getting caught.
- They do not promote good behaviour directly but simply serve to suppress misbehaviour.
- They do not deal with the cause of the misbehaviour.
- They focus attention on the misbehaviour.

Types of punishment

Despite the shortcomings of punishments, they do have a useful role to play in maintaining discipline if used skilfully. Each type of punishment has certain strengths and weaknesses which will have a bearing on their effectiveness. The most commonly used punishments are as follows.

- *Writing tasks.* These may range from writing out lines to a short essay on 'Why I misbehaved and will behave better in future'. The main advantage of this approach is that it is done in the pupil's own time without wasting yours. Its weakness is that it is often felt to have a patronising quality and is probably regarded as insulting by older pupils. It is essential not to require pupils to do work that is missing or overdue as a punishment. Doing schoolwork should not be a punishment. Such work must be explicitly justified on other grounds.

- *Detention*. This could entail keeping a pupil in detention for a break period or after school coupled with a writing task (as above) or simply detaining them in silence for a set period of time. Its main advantage is that it is widely disliked by pupils; its main disadvantage is that it can inconvenience you. It is essential to distinguish between a detention and requiring to see a pupil for a period of time as part of an investigating and counselling approach or to issue a reprimand. A detention is a formal punishment and should be administered as such.

- *Loss of privileges*. This can range from requiring a pupil to sit alone and in isolation to preventing the pupil going on a school outing. Its main advantage is that it can be quite upsetting to the pupil; its main disadvantage is that it can easily be seen as vindictive and unfair.

- *Exclusion from the class*. This can range from requiring the pupil to wait outside the classroom for a period of time to being sent to another classroom or place in the school. Its main advantage is that it removes the pupil from the classroom and allows them to think about why they were excluded; its main disadvantages are that it is not particularly unpleasant for some pupils and can pose other problems, such as a pupil who keeps looking in through a window or simply wanders off.

- *Verbal intimidation*. A very severe talking to may be considered as a punishment rather than a reprimand, particularly if done by a senior teacher in the school in a formal role. Its main advantages are that it can be very unpleasant and can be administered quickly; its main disadvantage is that it can provoke a confrontation. A severe talking to in this way should only take place in private.

- *Informing significant others*. Informing the headteacher or the pupil's parents is, for most pupils, very punishing. Its main advantage is that it is usually a quite powerful sanction; its main disadvantage is that the pupil may now feel labelled by the school as a disruptive pupil and may even feel the need to live up to this label as a result.

- *Symbolic punishment*. Some schools have a system of recording bad conduct marks which translate into a detention for a given total and may be included on the school report to parents. Its main advantage is that it can use the formal ritual of punishment at a mild level; its main disadvantage is that it can be clumsy to administer and communicate.

- *Exclusion from school*. This is the ultimate sanction. Exclusion can be temporary (usually one to five days in length) or permanent. It tends to be used as a final resort to help the pupil appreciate the immense gravity of the situation and the misbehaviour, either after a long history of problems or in reaction to a particular misbehaviour of the utmost seriousness (such as using drugs, or assaulting a teacher). For some, it provides the shock needed to salvage their school career or acts as a vehicle for the provision of special support. For others, it marks a point of no return. It may result in transfer to another school, with perhaps a fresh start. With pupils approaching the school leaving age, it may lead to a limbo land during which efforts to place the pupil elsewhere are finally overtaken by time running out.

Effective use of punishments

While it is evident that punishments generally have a more severe and unpleasant consequence for a pupil than strategies based on investigating and counselling or using reprimands, this does not mean that they are actually more powerful or effective in dealing with pupil misbehaviour. Research on the effectiveness of different strategies used to deal with difficult classes or pupils indicates that while almost any strategy can be effective if used skilfully in the right situation, generally strategies based on reasoning with pupils are the most effective. Indeed, recourse to a punishment in a situation may be counterproductive if all that might have been necessary and effective was offering some academic help or simply reasoning with the pupil. A major pitfall facing beginning teachers in particular, is to assume that a punishment is more powerful and hence more effective; as a result, they resort to their use too readily and inappropriately.

The skilful and effective use of punishments involves a number of qualities, and includes those considered earlier in relation to the effective use of reprimands. There are, however, some additional qualities worthy of particular note.

- *Sparing use.* Punishments should only be used sparingly and judiciously, and in the vast majority of cases only after other strategies have been tried.
- *Timing.* Punishments should be given as soon as possible after the misbehaviour. If there is a long delay, the link should be re-established at the time given.
- *Tone.* A punishment should be conveyed as an expression of your just and severe disapproval of the misbehaviour, and given in the interests of the pupil and of the class as a whole. It should not result from you losing your temper, or appear vindictive.
- *Fitting the crime.* The type and severity of the punishment should be appropriate to the misbehaviour but should also take account of the context.
- *Due process.* It is important that the pupil accepts that the punishment is fair and just. This will normally mean that the pupil has been warned that such a consequence may follow, and that your expectations and actions regarding such misbehaviour are clear and consistent. The pupil should also be asked to explain the misbehaviour and encouraged to understand and accept why the punishment is just, deserved and appropriate.
- *Relating to school policy.* The punishment should relate to the overall policy of the school towards discipline.
- *Aversiveness.* The punishment must be unpleasant for the pupil. Some pupils may not mind being sent out of the room, or may even gain status in the eyes of peers in doing so. As such, each punishment needs to be of a type that is aversive for the pupil concerned and minimises any factors that are likely to weaken its effectiveness, bearing in mind the need to be fair and consistent.

It is also important to consult with colleagues in the school about any pupil giving cause for concern. If a pupil is having to be punished frequently, this may indicate an underlying problem which goes well beyond being the concern of the class teacher alone. While you may feel you are expected to cope with any discipline problems yourself as best you can, this does not mean it is desirable to keep problems to yourself as far as possible. In fact, the opposite is the case. You also have a responsibility towards pastoral care and you need to act as a member of a team in monitoring pupils' behaviour, so that any concerns you have are shared with others and appropriate action can then be better and more widely informed.

Dealing with confrontations

From time to time, a confrontation may develop in the classroom between you and a pupil. A confrontation may be characterised by a heated and emotional exchange, which is upsetting for all concerned. Such a confrontation can develop so quickly and unpredictably, that the first thing you are aware of is that you are in the middle of having one. Usually, however, there are warning signals evident that enable you to pre-empt its development.

Triggers for confrontations

There are four major triggers for confrontation in the classroom:

- A pupil may feel emotional and tense as a result of prolonged learning difficulties which are causing increasing frustration.
- A pupil may feel that the disciplinary strategy you are adopting towards them is unfair and constitutes a threat to their self-esteem, particularly if linked to loss of face in front of their peers (the use of sarcasm or ridicule may provoke this, or trying to resolve a conflict by making the pupil submit to your authority in some way, such as moving to a seat at the front of the classroom).
- A pupil may react against explicit physical or verbal intimidation, such as a teacher waving a finger in front of the pupil's face or using a forceful reprimand.
- A pupil may be trying to avoid embarrassment when you are cajoling or insisting they answer a question or take part in an activity which they feel very anxious about, or in which they feel they may make a fool of themselves in front of others.

Clearly, skilful teaching and, in particular, the skilful use of the disciplinary strategies outlined earlier, will do much to minimise the occurrence of such triggers. However, there are circumstances which can lead to a pupil feeling over-sensitive to what otherwise would be unproblematic behaviour on your part. For example, the pupil may be having to deal with acute personal problems at home, or some upsetting news may have been received in school (e.g. being dropped from a school team, being told that their school report will be critical of poor progress, or even that a best friend has not invited the pupil to a party).

You can usually sense from a pupil's behaviour that something is amiss, such as the pupil looking tense or arriving in the classroom in an uncharacteristically loud manner. Such signals will alert you to the possibility that you may need to be sensitive to this in deciding how best to interact with the pupil.

Dealing with confrontations

If a confrontation does develop, there are some useful strategies that will enable you to deal successfully with the situation.

- *Stay calm.* If you remain calm, or regain your composure quickly, and interact calmly with the pupil, the pupil will quickly calm down.
- *Defuse the situation.* Rather than try to pursue the conflict further, you can tell the pupil that 'There's no need for anyone to get upset, I suggest you just calm down and we can deal with this at the end of the lesson' and then back off. If this is not effective, your best course of action is to send for help so that the pupil can be moved elsewhere for the rest of the lesson. Backing off in this way does not mean that you have backed down or lost authority. Indeed, it displays your skill in dealing with this as a special circumstance demanding appropriate action, and pupils will generally understand this. Some teachers can use humour to defuse a confrontation, but doing so successfully requires adept sensitivity.
- *Be aware of the heat of the moment.* A confrontation can develop in a matter of seconds, and in the heat of the moment you or the pupil may say or do something which they may profoundly regret later. Bear this in mind before you act and in how you respond to what the pupil says or does.
- *Use your social skills.* A pupil may be horrified by what they have said or done but may lack the social skills to get out of the situation. It thus behoves you to use your social skills to help the pupil, for which they may be immensely grateful later once the incident is defused and dealt with.
- *Design a mutual face-saver.* In the heat of the moment, your natural tendency may be to feel you must exert your authority by coming out 'on top' in some way. Such a stereotyped reaction is often unhelpful and counterproductive. You needs to consider which strategy best fits the situation, and enables you and the pupil to come away from the incident with sufficient grace
- *Get help if necessary.* Do not hesitate to get assistance from another member of staff if this seems appropriate.

Research on how teachers deal with confrontations indicates that almost all confrontations can be avoided or resolved by the skilful use of conflict management techniques. In particular, this requires teachers to be aware of their own emotions during conflicts and confrontations and how these might influence their behaviour, and to be able to stand outside the situation to think rationally about how best to proceed. The biggest danger facing you in dealing with a confrontation is to lose your temper or see the situation as 'I win – You lose' where you need to exert whatever power you have. By remaining calm, standing back from the situation, thinking carefully, and using appropriate strategies skilfully, the vast majority of such incidents can be defused and dealt with efficiently and effectively, and without becoming unnecessarily unpleasant.

Other strategies

As well as the strategies outlined so far, there are other strategies and approaches that are worthy of particular note.

Monitor your pupils' behaviour

Formal monitoring of behaviour

Formal procedures for monitoring pupils' behaviour can be effective. A frequently used strategy is to put a pupil 'on report', which means that for a period of a few days or a week, each teacher must make a note of the pupil's behaviour at the end of each teaching session on a report card. At the end of this period, the pupil's behaviour is reviewed.

Contracts

The notion of contracts involves promising the pupil an agreed reward of some type if good behaviour is maintained over a specified period. The reward may typically be a merit certificate for good behaviour, allowing the pupil to spend time on a valued activity (such as an afternoon in the craft workshop), or even a tangible reward (such as a bar of chocolate). It is important to note that the real motivation here does not stem from the desire for the reward, but rather the desire to behave well. The procedure and reward simply serve as a helpful vehicle to support the pupil's own efforts.

Getting help from parents and carers

Enlisting the help of pupils' parents and carers is often very important if the behaviour has become a serious cause for concern. Parents and carers should be informed about a cause for concern, not only as part of the desirability of keeping parents and carers informed in general about their children, but also because parents and carers may offer useful and helpful information themselves and assist in various ways to encourage an improvement in the pupil's behaviour. If it is suspected that the pupil may have a special educational need of some sort, then parents and carers should be involved in any discussions at an early stage.

The importance of the role of parents and carers is reflected in their inclusion in the TDA (2007) QTS standards, which refer to the need for student teachers to be able to communicate effectively with parents and carers and to recognise and respect the role that parents and carers can make to the development of pupils' well-being and to raising pupils' levels of attainment.

Units for disruptive pupils

Many schools are able to make use of on-site or off-site units to which disruptive pupils can be sent for a period of time. This can operate for quite short periods, such as one lesson, or half-a-day to provide a cooling-off period during which the pupil can come to terms with the gravity of the situation. In addition, it can operate for a longer period, perhaps three weeks, during which a detailed assessment and review of the pupils' behaviour and needs are considered. At its best, this strategy can allow a crisis to be defused successfully, followed by a return to normal schooling. At its worst, particularly for pupils near to the school-leaving age, it can result in *de facto* exclusion.

Positive teaching

Positive teaching refers to an approach to classroom discipline based on ideas stemming from behavioural psychology (McNamara, 2001; Porter, 2000). The basic underlying principle here is that pupil behaviour that is rewarded is more likely to occur in the same situation in future, and behaviour that is not rewarded or is punished, is less likely to occur. Advocates of this approach to classroom teaching argue that it enables teachers to be more consistent, systematic and effective in how they deal with discipline problems. First, the teacher needs to identify desirable behaviours that need to be promoted, and the types of misbehaviour that need to be discouraged. Having done this, you then use a programme of regularly praising and otherwise rewarding the desirable behaviours, and reminding pupils of the classroom rules that need to be adhered to. The important point about this approach is its emphasis on the use of praise and other rewards to encourage and sustain improved behaviour. Punishments are rarely used. Research studies based on evaluating this approach indicate that its skilful use can successfully improve the behaviour of the class as a whole and also promote better behaviour with individual pupils causing problems.

Further reading

Chaplain, R. (2003) *Teaching Without Disruption in the Primary School: A Model for Managing Pupil Behaviour.* London: RoutledgeFalmer. An insightful analysis of how to anticipate and manage pupil misbehaviour. [There is also a version of this book that focuses on secondary schools.]

Porter, L. (2000) *Behaviour in Schools.* Maidenhead: Open University Press. A useful account of different ways of looking at the nature and causes of pupil misbehaviour and their implications for how to promote good behaviour.

Rogers, B. (1998) *You Know the Fair Rule: Strategies for Making the Hard Job of Discipline and Behaviour Management in School Easier,* 2nd edn. London: Prentice Hall. This book presents a strategic approach to dealing with disruptive behaviour based on developing a repertoire of techniques that can be used consistently.

Rogers, B. (2006) *Classroom Behaviour: A Practical Guide to Effective Teaching, Behaviour Management and Colleague Support,* 2nd edn. London: Paul Chapman. An excellent guide to dealing with pupil misbehaviour.

Key questions about your use of discipline

1 Is my discipline embedded within a positive classroom climate characterised by mutual respect and rapport and positive expectations, and linked with good lesson presentation and management?
2 Is my authority established and accepted by pupils?
3 Am I clear and consistent in establishing rules and expectations regarding pupils' behaviour?
4 Do I make good use of general teaching skills and pre-emptive strategies to minimise pupil misbehaviour?
5 Do I make good use of investigating and counselling strategies, reprimands and punishments, to deal with pupil misbehaviour skilfully?
6 Are the strategies I use to deal with pupil misbehaviour employed flexibly and skilfully to take account of which strategy is likely to be most effective and appropriate to the situation?
7 Do my disciplinary strategies encourage good behaviour without undermining a positive classroom climate?
8 Do I avoid confrontations where possible, and efficiently and effectively diffuse those that do occur?
9 Am I sufficiently sensitive to my pastoral care role and alert to any particular needs of individual pupils giving cause for concern?
10 Do I make adequate use of consultation with colleagues and ensure that my actions complement the school's general policy towards discipline?

7 Assessing pupils' progress

The regular assessment of pupils' progress is part and parcel of teaching and learning in the classroom. Such assessment may range from simply looking over pupils' shoulders while they are writing during a period of classwork, to the use of formally administered external examinations. Indeed, there is a vast variety of activities used to assess pupils' progress, each with their own particular processes and procedures. Nevertheless, the skilful use of assessment techniques can be identified, and these will be highlighted in this chapter.

The phrase 'fitness for purpose' applies more importantly to assessment than to any other aspect of a teacher's work. Because assessment is very time consuming, it is very easy to find yourself spending hours collating records of assessment that you later realise you have no productive use for; or spending hours making detailed notes on pupils' test papers only to find later that pupils are given no opportunity to read and make use of these comments. Therefore the skilful matching of the type and the way you make use of a particular assessment activity to the key purpose that it is intended to serve is one of the key teaching skills.

The purposes of assessment

In essence, assessment is any activity used to appraise pupils' performance. The learning outcomes promoted by schools involve helping pupils to develop knowledge, understanding, skills and attitudes. Assessment thus consists of techniques you can use to monitor pupils' progress in terms of specific learning outcomes. The first and most important question facing you in assessing pupils' progress, is 'why'? What purpose have you in mind for the assessment activity?

Assessment can serve a number of different purposes. The most frequently used purposes are as follows.

- *To provide you with feedback about pupils' progress.* Such feedback enables you to consider how effective your teaching has been in achieving its intended learning outcomes. In particular, it may highlight certain problems or misunderstanding that have arisen, that will require remedial action in your subsequent teaching.
- *To provide pupils with educative feedback.* Assessment enables pupils to relate their performance to the standard expected, to use detailed feedback to correct and improve their work, and to appreciate more clearly the requirements of the tasks set (e.g. regarding the layout of the work or procedures used).
- *To motivate pupils.* Assessment activities can act as a spur to pupils to organise their work well and to learn what is required so as to achieve well at these activities. The spur may be largely based on intrinsic motivation, extrinsic motivation, or a mix of both. Feedback of success at a challenging task is particularly effective in stimulating future motivation.

- *To provide a record of progress.* Regular assessment activities enable you to keep a record of pupils' progress over a long period. This can then form the basis for your decisions about individual pupils' current and future educational needs, particularly if a cause for concern arises. It can also be used when communicating with others, including parents, and may influence your future planning of teaching similar groups.
- *To provide a statement of current attainment.* A specific assessment activity or group of activities can be used to identify the standard of attainment achieved at a particular point in time. Such attainment may form the basis of certification, or a formal statement issued to others, most notably parents.
- *To assess pupils' readiness for future learning.* Assessment can be used to indicate whether pupils are ready for a particular type of learning (e.g. readiness to learn to read), whether they have any specific learning difficulties, or, more simply, whether they have covered the previous learning required for the new topic to be taught effectively (if not, revision or prior preparation will be needed).
- *To provide evidence of teacher and school effectiveness.* Pupils' performance in assessment tasks provides evidence of their progress and hence acts as a useful indicator of teacher and school effectiveness.

Your decision about how and what to assess will thus depend on the exact purpose or purposes you have in mind for the assessment. Part of the difficulty facing teachers in making skilful and effective use of assessment is the need to meet different purposes and uses of assessment at the same time, and to ensure that any undesirable side-effects are avoided or limited as far as possible.

Dangers of assessment

There are three major dangers that you need to guard against when making use of assessment activities. First, and most serious of all, is the danger that pupils who find that the feedback concerning their progress indicates that they are doing less well than their peers or some standard of attainment of value to them, may become disheartened and upset by this. This may lead to their becoming disenchanted and alienated from schooling, and sinking into a vicious cycle of increasing underachievement. Second, the procedures and practices adopted for assessing pupils' progress may be too time-consuming and bureaucratic for teachers and pupils, so that they encroach undesirably on time and energy that could be better spent on other activities. Third, they may lead teachers and pupils to becoming over-concerned with pupils performing well. In particular, the lessons and assessment activities (both the content and the teaching and learning processes involved) may become geared to promoting success in attainment tests at the expense of the quality of educational experiences occurring in the classroom.

Because assessment practices are so interlinked with teaching and learning, the skilful use of assessment practices which complement and facilitate the hallmarks of effective teaching considered in previous chapters is essential. Where assessment practices are used which have undesirable side-effects, these can make it much more difficult to teach effectively. Indeed, many of the reforms in assessment practices over the years have stemmed precisely from the recognition of the important role of assessment in promoting effective teaching.

Briggs *et al.* (2003) have also made the important point that when assessing a task in which the pupil has used ICT, one needs to make a distinction between the quality of the pupil's use of ICT and the pupil's subject-related attainment. The pupil may well have used the ICT well, but this may not corresponded to the same level of attainment in the subject.

Types of assessment

As a result of the diversity in the type of assessment practices used in schools, a number of key terms are now frequently referred to (Clarke, 2005; Weeden *et al.*, 2002). The most important of these are as follows.

- *Formative assessment.* Assessment aimed to promote effective future learning by pupils. It may do this by giving pupils helpful feedback, or by giving you feedback or information that will enable you to meet the pupil's future learning needs more effectively. Typically, such assessment tends to identify errors, difficulties or shortcomings in the pupil's work and offer advice, guidance and information to improve future performance.

- *Summative assessment.* Assessment which identifies the standard of attainment achieved at a particular moment in time, normally carried out at the end of a period of instruction (e.g. end of term, end of course). The most typical examples of these are the grades used on school reports of attainment, or the results of external examinations.

- *Norm-referenced assessment.* The grading of each pupil's performance is related to the performance of others. For example, if a grade A is defined as the level of performance achieved by the top 10 per cent of the assessment cohort, this would mean that no matter how high or low the general standard of work produced was, the best 10 per cent (no more and no less) would always receive a grade A.

- *Criterion-referenced assessment.* The grading of each pupil's performance is judged in terms of whether a particular description of performance (the criterion) has been met. This means that all pupils who meet this criterion would be assessed as achieving the related grade, regardless of how other pupils performed. Typical examples of these are graded tests used in music, modern languages and mathematics, the use of grade-related criteria at GCSE, and the level of attainment in the National Curriculum.

- *Diagnostic assessment.* This overlaps with formative assessment, but specifically identifies learning difficulties or problems. Certain tests can be used to identify particular needs (e.g. dyslexia), and related to the statement of special educational needs.

- *Internal assessment.* Assessment activities which are devised, carried out and marked by the class teacher, and often used as part of their own programme of teaching.

- *External assessment.* Assessment activities devised by examiners outside the school, and usually also marked by external assessors, although in many cases marking can be done by the class teacher but is then checked ('moderated') by external assessors on a sample basis.

- *Informal assessment*. Assessment based on the observation of performance which occurs in the classroom as part of normal classroom practice.
- *Formal assessment*. Assessment made following prior warning that an assessment will be carried out. This normally allows the pupil an opportunity to revise and prepare for the assessment.
- *Continuous assessment*. Basing the final assessment of the standard of attainment achieved on pieces of assessment made over a long period of time.
- *Terminal assessment*. Basing the final assessment of the standard of attainment achieved on an assessment made solely at the end of the course or programme of work.
- *Objective assessment*. Assessment activities and associated marking schemes having extremely high agreement between assessors on the marks awarded. The best example of this is the use of multiple choice tests.
- *Subjective assessment*. Assessment activities based on a subjective and impressionistic judgement of a piece of work. An example of this would be judging a painting, a vignette of acting, or a piece of creative writing.
- *Process assessment*. Assessment of an ongoing activity, such as reading aloud a poem or designing and conducting an experiment, in which the assessment is based on direct observation of the performance while in progress.
- *Product assessment*. Assessment based on a tangible piece of work, such as an essay, project, model or examination script, submitted for the purpose of assessment.

Discussion about types of assessment typically considers contrasting pairs, most notably:

- formative versus summative
- norm-referenced versus criterion-referenced
- internal versus external
- informal versus formal
- continuous versus terminal
- objective versus subjective
- process versus product.

While this is often helpful, the nature of assessment practices is often such that a mixture of each contrasting pair is in fact involved. Thus, for example, one may imagine that an end-of-year school report was primarily a summative assessment, but inspection of its content may reveal many comments and pieces of information clearly intended to be formative. Similarly, an assessment scheme for marking a coursework project may claim to be primarily criterion-referenced, but close inspection may reveal aspects that are clearly norm-referenced. In tailoring your assessment practice to the purpose you have in mind, it is most important that the assessment is effective in meeting the needs you have for it. Over-concern with its purity, in terms of pigeon-holing its type, is likely to be unproductive.

Assessment for learning

The phrase 'assessment for learning' has been increasingly used to refer to the ways in which pupils and teachers can make use of assessment activities to gain a clearer understanding of the learning that has taken place to date and how pupils' future learning can best progress (Black *et al.,* 2003; Gardner, 2006). This phrase builds upon and extends the notion of formative assessment, and has also been included by the DfES (2005b) as an important strand of personalised learning. Gardner (2006) lists ten principles which underpin assessment for learning:

- It is part of effective teaching.
- It focuses on how pupils learn.
- It is central to classroom practice.
- It is a key professional skill.
- It is sensitive and constructive.
- It fosters motivation.
- It promotes understanding of goals and criteria.
- It helps learners know how to improve.
- It develops the capacity for self-assessment.
- It recognises all educational achievement.

Strong links have also been made between assessment for learning and personalised learning as part of the Every Child Matters agenda that has been developed by the DfES (2004b) to promote pupil achievement in schools (Cheminais, 2006). The particular importance of the skilful use of formative assessment in promoting motivation and learning is now widely recognised (O'Donnell *et al.,* 2007).

Improving assessment practices

Looking at the types of assessment listed above, and bearing in mind the range of *learning outcomes* that can be assessed (knowledge, understanding, skills and attitudes), the type and nature of the *performance involved* (oral, written, practical, coursework, tests, examinations) and the *educational domains* (academic subjects, study skills, personal and social education), it is perhaps not surprising that a number of complex issues underlie the skilful assessment of pupils' progress. Attempts to improve the nature and quality of assessment practices used in schools are continually evident in many countries.

The introduction of the National Curriculum in 1989 was coupled with associated procedures for monitoring pupils' progress involving the use of centrally produced tests. The results of these tests have been used both to provide an indication of each pupil's individual progress and an indication of the general progress made by pupils in each school compared with other schools. However, a number of problems and issues have emerged concerning the use of centrally produced National Curriculum tests, and the use of GCSE and A-level results in the form of 'league tables' to monitor standards and make judgements about relative school effectiveness (Gardner, 2006).

Value-added and baseline assessments

One major problem that has been highlighted in respect of using league tables based solely on giving the final level of attainment of each pupil is that such tables do not provide a fair indicator of a teacher's or a school's effectiveness; rather, what needs to be considered is each pupil's progress. 'Value-added' refers to the difference between a pupil's initial level of attainment and their final level of attainment. It is argued that by taking account of pupils' prior levels of attainment, we can see whether a teacher or school is performing better or worse than one would have expected. Such an initial assessment is called a 'baseline assessment'.

Many primary and secondary schools carry out baseline assessments for each new intake of pupils in the areas of language and literacy, mathematics, and personal and social development, based on the class teacher's observations of a range of classroom activities during pupils' first few months at the school or by making use of standardised tests developed for this purpose.

The use of data on pupils' initial levels of attainment, whether based on teacher assessments, standardised tests, or the results of National Curriculum tests, together with information about the general socio-economic circumstances of the pupils, allows comparisons to be made between teachers and schools based on measures of value-added. Nationally produced tables of pupil progress and attainment at each school now include information about value-added.

Skills in assessing pupils' progress

The importance of developing skills in the ability to assess pupils is recognised by its inclusion in various lists of the skills expected of teachers. For example, the TDA (2007) QTS standards include several elements regarding assessment by teachers:

- knowledge of the assessment requirements for the subjects/curriculum areas and age ranges they teach
- knowledge of a range of approaches to assessment, including the importance of formative assessment
- knowledge of how to use local and national statistical information to evaluate the effectiveness of their own teaching, to monitor their pupils' progress, and to raise their pupils' levels of attainment
- making use of a range of assessment, monitoring and recording strategies
- assessing the learning needs of pupils in order to set challenging learning objectives
- providing timely, accurate and constructive feedback on pupils' attainment, progress and areas for development.

Records of achievement

One of the criticisms of assessment made for many years was that pupils were often awarded a single mark or grade to indicate their attainment, and that this provided very little useful information to pupils and others (including parents, employers, and university admissions tutors). As a result, a major development in assessment practice over the years has been the introduction of ways in which a much fuller record of pupils' progress in a school could be recorded, including both academic and non-academic aspects.

This includes the introduction of documents that provide the pupil with a record of their achievements whilst at the school. These are typically given to pupils when they reach school-leaving age, and aim to include as full a range of their achievements during their school careers as possible, both academic and non-academic. A number of primary schools also produce such records. However, evaluation studies have indicated that teachers need to develop a host of new assessment practices and procedures, and to operate these skilfully, for these documents to be produced efficiently and with validity.

Portfolios of pupils' work

Another major development in assessment practice has been the need for teachers to build up a portfolio of pupils' work to exemplify certain standards, in order to assist teachers in their monitoring of pupils' progress and also to enable them to make reliable and valid judgements in any assessments they carry out. To foster this, a number of documents and materials have been produced for teachers to help improve consistency in teacher assessment by providing examples of standards of pupil work and performance at different levels and grades.

Assessment activities in the classroom

As discussed earlier, assessment activities are going on in schools all the time, ranging from asking pupils questions during classwork, to administering a formal written examination. In carrying out assessment activities, you need to be clear about the main purpose or purposes of the assessment and the type of assessment you want to use, as has been considered so far in this chapter. After this, you are then ready to think about how best to select, design and carry out the appropriate assessment activities themselves.

The main assessment activities in use in the classroom are:

- monitoring classwork activities
- designated assessment tasks integrated within classwork
- homework

You should use a wide range of assessment activities

- assessment tests designed by the teacher
- standardised tests
- National Curriculum tests
- formal examinations.

Monitoring classwork activities

Monitoring classwork activities is a central aspect of teaching, and is bound up with your decision-making about the progress of the lesson and the feedback you give to pupils to facilitate their learning. The most important aspects of such assessment are that you ensure that you regularly monitor the progress of all pupils (not just those who frequently demand or require more attention). Furthermore, your monitoring should be investigative and active, in the sense that you actively probe pupils' current understanding and difficulties rather than simply rely on this being drawn to your attention in some way. Many forms of assessment in common use now involve teachers monitoring pupil performance during classwork.

Designated assessment tasks integrated within classwork

There is a thin line between monitoring classwork activities and using designated assessment tasks integrated within classwork. Some activities that need to be assessed occur in classwork on a regular basis, whereas others need to be specifically designed and introduced for the purpose of the assessment. The latter is often the case if it is important for the task to be carefully standardised and assessed in terms of specific criteria that require close attention. In either case, however, you need to consider whether you should forewarn pupils that a particular assessment activity is to take place and indicate its purpose and use. Skilful assessment of pupils' progress in meeting the National Curriculum attainment targets depends very much on how well assessment tasks are integrated within classwork without disrupting or interfering unduly with the progress of learning.

As the range of activities within the classroom increases, so the range of assessment skills teachers need to develop also increases. For example, the skills needed to give formative assessment for a PowerPoint presentation and the skills needed to then assess the final product will be quite new for a teacher who has not taught and assessed such work before. A study by Postholm (2006) looked at the skills involved in the ways in which teachers can monitor and support pupils undertaking project work, encourage and help pupils to assess their own work and the work of other pupils, and in discussion with the pupil explain how the final grade for the finished piece of work was arrived at and justified. In particular, Postholm focused on the quality of the dialogue between the teacher and pupil, to illustrate how the teacher was able to help foster pupils' learning during the ongoing assessment of the project work they were undertaking.

Homework

The use of homework tasks is very important in providing feedback on how well a pupil can perform when unaided. Homework is particularly useful in developing pupils' organisational skills and power of commitment to meet the demands made on them.

It can also provide stark feedback to the pupil and to you on the nature of any difficulties or problems that arise which are less evident in the class where you may be readily available to provide help. Unfortunately, in this respect, parental help is useful in providing further tuition, but unhelpful if it readily enables the pupil to enlist assistance rather than persevere with their own efforts. Parental help has also posed problems for the assessment of independent project work done partly or largely at home, and much such work now has to be based solely on classwork activity.

It is common for homework to be used to assess pupils' previous learning in lessons, and often involves consolidation and practice-type tasks, or preparing for a test by revising. However, it is also important to use homework to good effect by encouraging new learning. This involves not simply the learning of new material, but also creative investigation and application of the topic area to life outside the school (e.g. listing cubes, spheres and cylinders that can be found in the pupil's living room, or exploring the earliest recollections of the pupil's parents about when they first went to school).

Assessment tests designed by the teacher

Short tests devised by you can motivate learning in preparation for the test, and provide a formal note of attainment in the test. Regular tests can be particularly useful in conveying the importance of making progress with new learning, but can also be very threatening. As such, they have to be used with sensitivity and in a way that will facilitate rather than discourage learning. Short tests vary immensely in type and form, ranging from a spelling test based on homework, to an end-of-course or topic test used to assess academic progress.

Standardised tests

Standardised tests are widely used to monitor progress and attainment in key areas of learning. Such tests are standardised by being given to a large number of pupils of a specific age (usually a nationwide sample), so that the score of pupils who are well above average, average, and well below average can be identified. Standardised tests are thus *norm-referenced* tests. Thereafter, when a pupil takes this test, it is easy to see how well they have performed on the test relative to an average pupil of the same age. Intelligence tests are standardised tests. The most commonly used standardised test in learning is for reading, where a pupil's score is normally given in terms of a reading age. For example, if a 10-year-old pupil takes the test and achieves a reading age of 12, that indicates that the pupil's reading level is comparable to the reading level of an average 12-year-old.

A range of other standardised tests in learning include language tasks, mathematics, and tests used as part of screening procedures to identify pupils who may have special educational needs. Such tests are useful in enabling the teacher to compare the result with that expected for a pupil of that age. In using standardised tests, however, you must be alert to their appropriateness for the use you are making of them. In particular, a dated test may well include words, formats or tasks that are no longer commonly used. A mathematics test may explore attainment based on a different coverage or approach to the one your pupils have experienced. In addition, a test result, of course, can only be based on what was tested, which means that other aspects of performance which may be difficult to test are largely excluded. Given the increasing diversity of learning skills and qualities being fostered in schools, written tests in particular are likely to be inadequate as the major or sole assessment activity used to measure attainment.

National Curriculum tests

National Curriculum tests are designed to test whether a pupil can perform as described in terms of the levels of the National Curriculum attainment targets. Such tests are thus *criterion-referenced* tests.

Formal examinations

Formal examinations devised by the school are a common feature of school life. The formality varies from classroom-based examinations designed and administered by the class teacher at an appropriate time, to examinations designed in collaboration and administered as part of an examination timetable. As well as providing a useful measure of attainment to be used in school reports, they also help pupils to develop examination skills and techniques which prepare pupils for externally set tests and examinations.

Making use of local and national data on pupil attainment for target setting

Data are available to enable teachers and schools to compare pupil attainment in their own class and school with the standards of pupil attainment achieved locally and nationally. They can also do this in a way that enables them to make comparisons with those schools that have a similar intake of pupils (in terms of their range of ability and the type of community catchment they serve). Such comparisons enable teachers and schools to set sensible targets for raising standards.

Carrying out assessment activities

In carrying out assessment activities, a number of important points need to be borne in mind:

- The assessment activity must be a fair one, in the sense of relating to the work covered, so that pupils can be reasonably expected to perform well on the activity if progress has been made during the appropriate coursework.
- The assessment activity should relate to the learning outcomes planned by the school, which may be documented in terms of appropriate aspects of the National Curriculum or as part of a particular course of study detailing syllabus, content and assessment criteria to be achieved.
- The programme of assessment activities used over a long period should be varied in type and form so that the full range of learning outcomes intended are assessed, and assessed in different ways.
- Pupils should be informed about the nature and purpose of assessment activities, how they are used, and the criteria employed that characterise successful performance.

- Assessment activities should be conducted in a manner that facilitates performance, by taking place in appropriate circumstances and, in particular, avoiding disruptions and, so far as possible, minimising pupils' anxieties.
- Assessment activities should be carefully designed to ensure that tasks are unambiguous and the type and nature of performance expected is clear to pupils.
- Most importantly of all, you need to ensure that the assessment activity actually assesses validly what it is intended to assess.

Skills underlying assessment

Three examples will suffice to illustrate the complex skills needed to carry out assessment activities effectively. The first example concerns designing a multiple-choice test in science. Consider the following question:

- In very cold weather, pipes sometimes burst because:
  (a) Water expands when it freezes.
  (b) Ice is harder than water.
  (c) Unlagged pipes always burst.
  (d) Cold water softens pipes.

In designing this item, the teacher needs to check that the question is clear and appropriate, and that the four options will effectively discriminate between pupils who have the understanding being tested from those who do not. You also need to consider whether this test item is a good example of the particular learning outcome being assessed: knowledge, understanding, ability to relate science to real-life applications, appreciation of the nature of cause and effect, or whatever.

A second example comes from a document to be completed by secondary school pupils taking part in a paired-reading scheme at a primary school as a component of a community studies course (paired reading involves the older pupil listening to the younger pupil's reading). The following section appears within the self-assessment section:

- When you have finished your module, we would like you to give a summary of your experience (please ring round the words to answer the questions).
  (a) Do you think the help you gave in reading was:
      useless, easy, exciting, useful, dull, enjoyable, difficult?
  (b) Do you think your attitude and behaviour was:
      responsible, unhelpful, helpful, wasting time?
  (c) Do you feel proud that you have done your best?
      yes, no, not sure
  (d) Would you like to do this type of thing again?
      yes, no, not sure

In designing this assessment activity, the teacher clearly needs to think about its purpose, whether it will do what it is intended to do effectively, and how it will be used. In particular, were the pupils involved in the design of this self-assessment section and informed of its purpose and use, and how will it be related to other evidence of their performance?

The third example is asking a class of junior school age pupils to write a short story about someone who fell into a river. Such a task could be used to assess a whole range of aspects on progress in writing, including technical aspects such as handwriting, grammar, punctuation and use of capital letters, and aspects of its content, such as creativity, use of ideas, and intelligibility to the reader. Because the same assessment task can be used for different areas of evaluation, it is often important to indicate to pupils which aspect is being assessed. Thus, for example, you could tell pupils to try and make the story as imaginative as possible, as this is the aspect you are assessing (hence a very imaginative story should still get a high mark even if there are technical shortcomings).

It will be evident from consideration of these three examples that carrying out assessment activities involves a whole range of skills regarding selection, design, implementation, match of activity to purpose, marking procedures, feedback, and appropriate and valid use of the results of the assessment.

Marking, recording and reporting

A number of studies and reports concerning assessment practices in primary and secondary schools have highlighted the importance of sound and appropriate practice regarding the marking of pupils' work and the recording and reporting of pupils' progress (Tanner, 2003). The way in which pupils' work is marked, recorded and reported has a major impact on pupils' subsequent motivation and the effort and strategies they use regarding further learning. As such, the skills displayed by a teacher in this area are of crucial importance.

Marking classwork and homework

The marking of pupils' work during and after lessons needs to be thorough and constructive, and the work should be returned in good time. Good practice in marking acts as an important model for pupils in setting them an example of the care and attention that needs to be devoted towards academic tasks, and can thereby maintain a high expectation for the standard of work required. The formative aspect of marking is of fundamental importance to effective teaching and learning. Feedback that enables the pupil to make further progress by understanding more clearly what needs to be done can enhance motivation and self-confidence. For example, receiving a low mark for the imaginative quality of an essay or for a description of an experimental procedure without any guidance as to how the work could have been improved, will tend to dishearten. Constructive and helpful guidance on how a better piece of work could have been produced will help stimulate further progress.

The marking of pupils' work completed as part of classwork and homework tasks is simply an extension of the normal process of teaching and learning. The major challenge facing you in marking pupils' work is how to be helpful and encouraging for the whole range of attainment in the class. The main problem is that norm-referenced marking, based on comparing the work of pupils with each other, will tend to discourage the lower attainers. Most teachers therefore try to make greater use of marking related to attainment standards expected of each pupil, taking account of previous progress. In this respect, good use can be made of tasks that are more clearly matched to each pupil's ability or using tasks which are graded in terms of increasing difficulty. In addition, you may decide to keep the written record of marks in your own record books but not report these to pupils. Instead, your feedback to pupils will take the form of comments about the work, and areas of improvement that are required. It is also important to give feedback about effort, if you feel a pupil has done less well or better than expected as a result of their efforts.

It is also helpful to make use of a variety of marking methods, including allowing pupils to mark their own work or each other's from time to time. In addition, marks over a period of time should be based on a variety of assessment activities to ensure that the run of marks reflects different aspects of attainment. The most important function of marking to bear in mind is that it should provide helpful and encouraging feedback to pupils about their progress. In part this may involve helping pupils to think about their study skills and how they organise their work so that they can better prepare for such assessment tasks in future.

The importance of developing the skills involved in assessing pupils' work is highlighted in a study by Smith and Gorard (2005). The increasing advocacy of the positive impact of formative assessment on pupils' learning has led many schools to place much greater emphasis on providing pupils with more detailed formative feedback on their work. One school studied by Smith and Gorard sought to take this one step further by exploring whether giving pupils formative feedback without an overall grade or mark would be more effective in promoting pupil attainment. Smith and Gorard found that the use of the 'formative feedback only' approach showed no evidence of being more effective, and in some areas of the data on pupil attainment appeared to be less effective. However, what was perhaps most evident from the study were apparent shortcomings in the quality of the formative feedback given at this school. The study highlights how a school cannot simply take what is advocated to be good practice 'off the shelf' and apply it at their own school; rather the teachers involved have to develop the necessary understanding and skills underpinning the practice being adopted.

Marking formal assessment tasks

As well as marking classwork and homework, you will also be marking a whole range of formal assessment tasks, including tests and examinations. The skills involved in such marking have become increasingly complex with the growth of more detailed marking practices. Performance in a subject or area of the curriculum is now typically divided into a number of components or elements, and the marking scheme is devised so that the mark awarded on a particular aspect of performance is clearly related to the component or element being assessed. This enables attainment to be recorded in terms of a profile of components rather than as an overall single mark or grade, or if the latter is the case, the single mark or grade is based on a specified weighting of the different components involved. For example, assessing a practical project might involve making a separate assessment on each of three stages involved: (i) planning the project, (ii) carrying out the project and analysing the data collected, and (iii) drawing conclusions.

The marking of formal tasks thus involves careful consideration, not so much of the correctness of the pupil's performance, but rather a judgement of what the quality of the performance indicates. The National Curriculum specifies for each subject area a number of attainment targets, which together make up the knowledge, understanding and skills that constitute increasing educational attainment. Each attainment target is divided into a number of levels to represent increasing attainment. Designing and marking the associated assessment tasks thus requires a clear appreciation of how performance relates to a specific level of attainment on the attainment target being assessed.

Thus, for example, the statement of attainment in science for a particular attainment target at a particular level might require pupils to be able to measure variations in living organisms. The task used to measure this must carefully take account of what precise type of pupil performance would exemplify this statement. To achieve this, the task needs to reflect a clear understanding of what the statement means and how it relates to this particular attainment target at the specified level; it also needs to incorporate a mark scheme for performance that is fair, reliable, valid and practical.

Marking personal qualities and attitudes

The assessment of personal qualities and attitudes has always posed problems of reliability and validity. Whilst most teachers form impressionistic judgements about personal qualities and attitudes, some forms of assessment, such as Records of Achievement, have demanded that teachers' judgements be based on performance related to particular tasks where a fair opportunity to display particular qualities or attitudes (such as acting responsibly, showing initiative, working conscientiously when unsupervised) can be given. Again, it is important to prepare pupils for such assessment and to discuss with them what is expected, and how marks or grades are achieved.

Recording pupils' progress

The need for teachers to keep good records of pupils' progress has been emphasised frequently by Ofsted in their inspections of schools. However, it is also important to recognise that the usefulness of keeping records is dependent on the extent to which the records are in fact used. Keeping records that are much too detailed or in a form that serves little purpose will not be a good use of your time.

Keeping a good record of pupils' progress should serve three main functions:

- It should provide a useful basis from which reports to others (e.g. the pupils themselves, parents, other teachers, other establishments) can be made.
- It should highlight any cause for concern if a pupil's performance shows a marked drop compared with previous progress.
- It should facilitate the planning of future work with each pupil by building upon previous progress and, in particular, by ensuring that progress is adequate in its breadth and depth of coverage and that areas requiring remedial work receive attention.

Keep thorough records of your pupils' progress

In addition, such records can usefully contribute to the school's general decision-making about its own effectiveness and coverage of the programmes of study. In this respect, notes about the work covered, including samples of pupils' work and test scores, can help to ensure that the curriculum provided each year matches pupils' needs and abilities adequately.

Reporting pupils' progress

Feedback to pupils about their progress is of immense importance in contributing to motivation and further progress, as has been noted already. However, you also need to report on pupils' progress on a regular basis to parents and carers, both in the form of written reports and during meetings with them.

Written reports to parents have been the subject of much debate. On the one hand parents typically complain that they would like to receive reports more frequently, in more detail, and for reports to be more meaningful. On the other hand, teachers complain that producing such reports is very time-consuming and involves a number of problems that are not easy to resolve. For example, there is a tension between giving honest reports and avoiding demoralising pupils or parents if the comments are critical or reflect low attainment; in addition, it is difficult to summarise performance in a way that is concise but which parents can easily understand.

Writing reports that are fair, valid, meaningful to the reader, and have a positive effect on future progress involves a number of skills. As well as making good use of your knowledge about each pupil and your records of progress, you need to make comments that are helpful and constructive. Where you need to be critical, this should usefully point to what needs to be done in future to improve matters. In addition, school reports need to adhere to relevant national guidance on their content and format.

Further reading

Black, P., Harrison, C., Lee, C., Marshall, B. and Wiliam, D. (2003) *Assessment for Learning: Putting it into Practice.* Maidenhead: Open University Press. An excellent overview of the 'assessment for learning' approach.

Gardner, J. (ed.) (2006) *Assessment and Learning.* London: Sage. An excellent analysis of the issues involved in considering how the 'assessment for learning' approach can contribute to improved classroom practice.

Tanner, H. (2003) *Marking and Assessment.* London: Continuum. This book offers a succinct and helpful overview of key issues concerning assessment and offers advice on how best to address these.

Weeden, P., Winter, J. and Broadfoot, P. (2002) *Assessment: What's in it for Schools?* London: RoutledgeFalmer. An excellent analysis of the skills that underpin effective assessment linked with the promotion of pupils' learning.

Key questions about your assessment of pupils' progress

1 Do I make use of an appropriate variety of assessment activities?
2 Do I make use of the various purposes for assessment, including both formative and summative purposes and also as means of monitoring the success of my own teaching and further planning?
3 Do I ensure that each assessment activity is well tailored to the purpose for which it is intended?
4 Is my marking of assessment tasks and feedback to pupils sufficiently speedy, thorough, constructive and helpful, so as to foster and sustain pupils' motivation and self-confidence and facilitate further progress?
5 Do I help pupils to prepare for assessment tasks so as to enable them to achieve success by having a clear understanding of the expectations required and how these can best be achieved?
6 Are the assessment activities I use fair in terms of being well matched to the work covered and to pupils' abilities, and in terms of being valid indicators of the learning outcomes being monitored?
7 Are the assessment activities carried out in a way that will facilitate achievement?
8 Do I help develop pupils' ability to evaluate their own progress through the use of self-assessment activities?
9 Are my records of pupils' progress based on a variety of types of assessment activities and different aspects of performance, and are they well suited to the purposes for which the records are kept?
10 Are my reports to parents, and others, fair and informative?

8 Reflection and evaluation

All teachers spend a great deal of time reflecting on and evaluating how well they are performing, both with particular regard to their classroom teaching and to other aspects of their work in general. Reflection and evaluation are inherent in the job and are an essential part of developing your teaching skills (Bubb, 2004; Jacklin *et al.*, 2006; Leach, 2006). Indeed, the TDA (2007) QTS standards highlight the importance of student teachers being able to:

- evaluate the impact of their teaching on the progress of all pupils, and modify their planning and classroom practice where necessary
- reflect on and improve their practice and take responsibility for identifying and meeting their developing professional needs
- identify priorities for their early professional development in the context of induction.

It is impossible to meet the various demands of teaching without planning, organising and evaluating the activities you carry out. What differs between teachers, however, is how skilfully and systematically they carry this out.

Over the years, this quality of critically thinking about your own performance in the classroom, often referred to as 'reflective teaching' (Pollard *et al.*, 2005), has been widely advocated as needing to be fostered and encouraged as part of teachers' normal practice and professional development.

All teachers do this in an intuitive and *ad hoc* way most of the time. However, some teachers have also been involved in more systematic self-appraisal processes, either as part of a specific scheme of self-evaluation within the school, or as part of a network of teachers who have been involved in researching aspects of their own practice within the teacher action research movement (Costello, 2003; Koshy, 2005).

Working with other teachers as part of a learning community is increasingly recognised as being a powerful and effective way of enabling teachers to reflect upon and develop their classroom practice. Indeed, the TDA (2007) QTS standards highlight the importance of student teachers being able to:

- have a creative and constructively critical approach towards innovation, being prepared to adapt their practice where benefits and improvements are identified
- have a commitment to collaboration and co-operative working
- act upon advice and feedback and be open to coaching and mentoring
- work as a team member and identify opportunities for working with colleagues, sharing the development of effective practice with them
- ensure that colleagues working with them are appropriately involved in supporting learning and understand the roles they are expected to fulfil.

In addition, the establishment of formal schemes of teacher appraisal (Jones *et al.*, 2006; Middlewood and Cardno, 2001) and the publication of guidance for schools on how school inspectors evaluate the quality of classroom teaching, have contributed to the extent to which teachers are engaged in regularly and systematically reflecting on their own classroom practice.

Teachers also need to continuously update and develop their understanding of subject matter, and how these can be taught in the classroom, as well as their knowledge and understanding of how pupils learn and develop, and how pupil learning can be affected by a variety of developmental, social, religious, ethnic, cultural and linguistic influences. Whilst some initial grounding in these areas will be established during initial teacher training, as noted by their inclusion in the TDA (2007) QTS standards, these need to be revisited in the light of new research findings, as well as in the light of changes in policies.

For example, the Every Child Matters agenda (Cheminais, 2006; DfES, 2004b) has placed new requirements on teachers to update their understanding of:

- the legal requirements and policy concerning the well-being of pupils
- how best to support pupils whose progress, development and well-being is affected by changes or difficulties in their personal circumstances
- when to refer pupils to colleagues for specialist support.

Whilst these requirements are reflected in the TDA (2007) QTS standards, they also have important implications for the development of new practice amongst established teachers.

Self-evaluation

There are two key aspects of self-evaluation. First, what aspects of your teaching need to be considered in order to improve your future practice? Second, how can you best go about improving your practice in the area that could usefully be developed? The first aspect thus involves setting yourself, or being set by others, an agenda about classroom teaching to consider, and then collecting some data that will enable you, or others, to judge the area that could usefully be developed. The second aspect deals with the programme for development.

Setting an agenda for classroom teaching

The initial agenda for your classroom teaching can be set in a number of ways. Studies of teacher self-evaluation indicate that most teachers tend to take as their starting point some problem that they are concerned about, rather than attempt to formally review their teaching as a whole. For example, a teacher may feel that they ought to make greater use of group-work activities, or that coursework activities need to be more clearly planned, or that too many pupils in the class become restless and inattentive during lessons. Such concerns may lead the teacher to explore carefully their own current practice with a view to considering how best to improve future practice. This process would constitute the first part of a teacher action research strategy, which would then lead on to devising a solution to improve practice, implementing the solution, and then evaluating its success.

Teachers who attempt to review their teaching as a whole are usually involved in a formal scheme of some sort, in which a checklist of questions about current practice or a set of rating scales are used. For example, the following list of statements is fairly typical as a means of stimulating a teacher's reflections on their current classroom practice. The teachers are asked to rate themselves on each statement as either 'I am happy with this aspect of my teaching' or 'I think I could usefully look at this aspect further'. The statements are:

- I plan my lessons well, with clear aims and a suitable lesson content and structure.
- I prepare the materials needed for the lessons, such as worksheets and apparatus, in good time.
- My explanations and instructions are clear and pitched at the right level for pupils to understand.
- I distribute questions around the classroom well and use both open and closed questions.
- I use a variety of learning activities.
- My lessons are suitable for the range of ability of pupils in the class (able, average, less able).
- I maintain a level of control and order that is conducive for learning to occur.
- I monitor pupils' learning closely during the lesson and give help to those having difficulties.
- I mark work, including homework, thoroughly, constructively and in good time.
- I have good relationships with pupils based on mutual respect and rapport.
- My subject expertise is fine for the work I do.

In order to help ensure that teachers are honest in using this list of statements, they are told that it is for their personal use, simply to help them think about which areas of their classroom teaching they might like to focus on as part of the self-evaluation or teacher appraisal process. It is useful to note that the second rating category is carefully worded so that it does not imply that by wanting to look at this aspect further, your current practice is unsatisfactory. This is essential, since the need for change in your teaching often has nothing to do with your current practice being weak, nor does it mean your previous practice was wrong. Not appreciating this point has caused many teachers faced with the need to change much unnecessary anguish.

Rating scales

As well as such checklists, many teachers have made use of more sophisticated rating scales in the role of appraiser when observing the teaching of a colleague. Such classroom observation instruments vary greatly in format and content, and in particular whether the rating scale is norm-referenced (e.g. above average, average, below average) or criterion-referenced (i.e. describes the behaviour indicative of each category on the rating scale), or a judgemental and ambiguous mixture of both (e.g. outstanding, good, average, poor).

There is no definitive description of what constitutes effective teaching, as was noted in Chapter 1. Therefore a whole variety of different classroom observation instruments have been used to explore classroom practice, including those devised by government agencies, researchers, teacher trainers, and schools. The ways in which such observation schedules have been used have also varied. At one extreme are observers who maintain a detached stance by sitting at the back of the classroom for the whole lesson, whilst at the other extreme are those who frequently circulate around the room at appropriate times, talk to pupils, look at pupils' work, and even assist with the lesson when possible. What is of crucial importance in the use of such rating scales is that they lead to an informative and constructive dialogue between the observer and the observed that helps to stimulate the quality of the latter's thinking about their own classroom practice.

Using an agreed list of teaching skills

Over the years, many attempts have been made by government agencies to clearly define the teaching skills that should be developed during the course of initial teacher training, and which should then develop further during a teacher's career supported by appropriate in-service education and other professional development activities.

Unfortunately the main problem with such attempts is that they tend to emphasise the summative assessment aspects of teaching skills rather than the formative aspects, thereby implying that the main aim of teacher appraisal and school inspection is to identify weaknesses that need development. As was noted earlier, however, the need of most teachers to develop their classroom practice is more to do with the requirement to meet new demands stemming from changes in the curriculum and patterns of teaching, learning and assessment, than to correct weaknesses. Teacher appraisal and school inspection schemes need to emphasise the formative aspects of appraisal and provide a supportive ethos that will foster and encourage teachers' own reflection and evaluation about their classroom teaching if such schemes are to facilitate teachers' efforts to monitor and develop their own classroom practice.

Portfolios and profiles

One of the means by which teacher training courses aim to encourage student teachers to reflect regularly on their classroom practice is to require them to build up a portfolio of their teaching based on their lesson plans, their notes on how the lessons went, and feedback from observation of their lessons by course tutors and school mentors. Some teacher training courses also make use of a variety of profiling documents to comment on individual lessons and to record student teachers' progress during the training course, both with respect to the general classroom teaching and to more specific aspects, such as the use of a profiling document to record students' development of skills in the use of information technology.

Induction as a newly qualified teacher

One of the benefits of building up a portfolio and having a profile of one's skills at the end of initial teacher training is that such documents can form a very useful basis from which to consider your professional development needs during the first few years as a qualified teacher. Indeed, many schools have a well-established programme to support newly qualified teachers during their first year of appointment (the induction year), in which opportunities to review their progress and their development needs are provided. This is coupled with having another teacher in the school formally appointed to be your mentor, and to whom you can go for advice and guidance. The career entry and development profile completed at the end of the initial teacher training programme is designed to help make the induction year programme more effective.

Research on the experience of beginning teachers during the induction year has highlighted the importance of the quality of mentoring that new teachers receive to enable their confidence and teaching skills to develop. A study by Kyriacou and Kunc (2007) tracked a group of beginning teachers over a three-year period, covering their PGCE year and their first two years in post. The quality of mentoring they received in schools had a major impact on the progress they felt they made in the development of their teaching skills.

Becoming an expert teacher

The growth of expertise in classroom teaching is clearly crucial for your professional growth and for the effectiveness of the whole school system. Much attention has consequently been paid to how teachers can be helped to develop and extend their teaching skills and to meet the demands for changes in their classroom practice that must inevitably occur from time to time. Unfortunately, as teachers develop greater expertise, they are also likely to gain promotion to posts that involve more administrative work and less classroom teaching, with the result that some of the best classroom teachers gradually do less teaching as their careers develop. One way of mitigating this is to establish a grade of expert teacher, which enables a teacher to gain a promoted post (with additional pay) whilst retaining a full classroom teaching load.

The establishment by the DfES of 'threshold' standards for experienced teachers seeks to recognise and reward the development of teacher expertise and the significant contribution that such teachers make to the school through the quality of their teaching and the wider role they play in the work of the school. The threshold standards cover:

- knowledge and understanding
- teaching and assessment
- pupil progress
- wider professional effectiveness
- professional characteristics.

The threshold standards add to the QTS standards and the induction standards. Meeting the threshold standards enables teachers to earn a consolidated pay increase and to have access to further points on their pay scale.

The DfES has also established two further sets of standards: one for the 'advanced skills teacher' and the other for the grade of 'excellent teacher'. Teachers awarded these two grades are expected to take a leading role in the development of the classroom practice of teachers at their own and at other schools. The threshold standards, the advanced skills teacher standards, and the excellent teacher standards, all require the teacher to provide evidence that their teaching has led to higher pupil attainment.

Defining the skills of an expert teacher, however, has been particularly problematic (Berliner, 1995). It is easy to assume that expert teachers are simply teachers who display the same range of skills as 'competent' teachers, only more so. However, research on the differences between expert teachers and other teachers reveals that expert teachers appear to have additional qualities that go beyond those displayed by other teachers. These additional qualities seem to be:

- a commitment to their work that goes well beyond the call of duty
- some degree of charisma that flows from the quality of their interest in the work they do and in the pupils they teach
- an insightful grasp of the essence of what needs to be learned and how best to get pupils from where they are now to where they need to be
- an insightful ability to anticipate problems and to intervene effectively when problems do occur so that pupils' learning can progress smoothly.

Responding to new pedagogies

All teachers need to develop new skills in response to changes in pedagogy. Developments such as the National Strategies (Webb, 2006), the extension of inclusive education (Avramidis, 2006) and new ICT technologies (Gillespie, 2006) have all had a major impact on how teachers teach, giving rise to 'new pedagogies'. This has highlighted the importance of teachers' ability to reflect upon their professional development needs and to take the action needed to develop new teaching skills in response to the new pedagogies. MacBeath (2006) notes that school inspections by Ofsted now place much greater emphasis on the role played by school and teacher self-evaluation in contributing to the development of those teaching skills that underpin high-quality teaching in response to new pedagogies.

The TDA (2007) QTS standards acknowledge the importance of student teachers needing to have a secure knowledge and understanding of their subjects/curriculum area, and related pedagogy within the context of the relevant curricula frameworks. Such knowledge and understanding, however, needs to be continually developed and updated. For example, the incorporation of the Every Child Matters agenda into the QTS standards is reflected by the requirement that student teachers need to be aware of issues concerning the safeguarding and promotion of pupils' well-being.

Collecting data about your current practice

Whatever the circumstances are in which you come to appraise your classroom teaching, whether self-initiated or as part of a formal scheme of appraisal, and whether using a list of teaching skills and some type of observation schedule or not, you will need to consider detailed information about aspects of your teaching if you are to base your plans for further development on a systematic analysis of your current practice. Collecting and receiving such feedback is the area we turn to next.

During a period when there are major changes in the curriculum relating to patterns of teaching, learning and assessment, it will be relatively clear from the new demands

Collect as much information as you can about your classroom practice

made on you what areas of your current practice will need to be developed. It may be that as a primary school teacher you will need to develop your teaching of science or history topics, or as a secondary school teacher to develop your teaching of investigational work in mathematics or assessment of coursework tasks in English.

However, it is just as important during periods when major changes are not taking place in the curriculum, for you to be able to undertake self-initiated reflection on your current practice, with a view to thinking about aspects of your teaching which you are broadly happy with but which nevertheless might usefully merit attention. It is in exploring your current practice during such periods when there is no obvious problem or demand for you to change your practice, that collecting data in some way can be particularly helpful.

Methods of data collection

There are a variety of ways in which you can collect data about your current practice. One or more of the following methods are likely to be the most useful.

- *Writing a diary.* This may be done after each lesson with a particular class or classes or alternatively at the end of each school day. It can be particularly useful in helping you to clarify the nature of your concerns and in noting particular incidents which are examples of the concern.
- *Making a recording of your lessons.* This may be done using an audiotape or a videotape. The main advantage of such recordings is that their detail enables you to highlight aspects of your teaching which, during the busy-ness of the actual lessons, you are unaware of as being worthy of attention and development.
- *Getting feedback from a colleague observing your lessons.* This is an essential feature of formal schemes of teacher appraisal, but has also featured widely in many informal co-

operative activities amongst teachers exploring their own practice. Feedback from an observer appears to work best when you brief your observer about the aspect of your teaching you want feedback on, and when such feedback is descriptive (i.e. describes what happened) rather than judgemental. Judgemental feedback is also valuable, but great care needs to be taken to ensure that the judgement comes from a trusted observer, occurs in a supportive and non-threatening context, and is fair. Interestingly, observers often claim to learn as much, if not more, about their own teaching from observing colleagues, as from being observed themselves. Schemes that involve teachers observing each other have thus been particularly successful in stimulating teachers' thinking about their own teaching.

- *Getting feedback from pupils*. You can get useful feedback from pupils in a number of ways. You could ask pupils to write a diary about your lessons. In some cases this has been used to encourage pupils to reflect upon their learning experiences linked to a personal and social education programme or records of achievement. You could ask pupils to complete a questionnaire about your lessons, which explores aspects of your teaching and their experience of learning. You could interview pupils individually, or in groups, or hold a class discussion. Studies that have looked at teachers' use of feedback from pupils to evaluate their teaching have invariably found that such feedback is very valuable and of high quality, and that the main reluctance by many teachers to solicit such feedback seems to be more to do with a fear that it may undermine the authority inherent in their role rather than with concerns about its quality.

Many teachers have made use of a mixture of methods for data collection, and once you have focused more clearly on the particular aspect of your classroom teaching you wish to explore, the data collection can be made sharper and more specific. For example, a year 8 class teacher in a junior school used a diary, observations and an audiotape to explore how well pupils set about various tasks. As a result, he noticed that because he organised the learning activities so that pupils had to complete an English or a mathematics task before they could move on to 'more exciting' tasks, such as art or project work, some pupils simply rushed the first task. Furthermore, pupils with difficulties tended to become frustrated because they could not finish the first task in good time. He then introduced a rotating timetable in which the first task lasted for a specified length of time. This relieved the pressure on pupils, and on him, and the new organisation of the activities led to an improvement in the quality of the work produced and in the pupils' attitudes and motivation towards the work.

Ideas for reflection

A number of writers have produced texts aimed at helping teachers to reflect upon some aspect of their classroom practice by carrying out practical activities that will provide some useful data with which to analyse their teaching (Neil and Morgan, 2003; Pollard *et al.*, 2005). Examples of areas that might be addressed in this way are:

- obtaining a 'measure' of the classroom climate
- exploring your use of classroom rules

- exploring how pupils feel about particular topics
- monitoring a particular child's curricular experiences for one week
- examining tasks in terms of their learning demands
- investigating question-and-answer sessions
- evaluating the techniques you use to assess pupils' progress
- reviewing the motivational qualities of different activities
- looking at the quality of your relationships with pupils
- examining the time pupils spend on different types of activities
- reviewing the work you set for the more able pupils
- reviewing your use of information technology activities.

Many of these activities can be carried out by the teacher acting alone and making use of appropriate materials, whilst others may require the assistance of colleagues. Indeed, one interesting development in schools has been an increase in the sharing of ideas and data about one's own teaching with colleagues, as part of a collaborative scheme in which teachers try to explore aspects of their own practice. Such schemes may involve a small group of teachers at a particular school, or a small group of teachers from different schools. In addition, many in-service workshops for teachers are now based around the collecting and sharing of data about the development of their practice during a specified period, lasting say one academic year, during which each teacher focuses on and develops one particular aspect of the classroom teaching. Unlike traditional in-service workshops, which tend to be one-off sessions involving inputs from 'experts', this approach means that the development is initiated, developed and sustained over a long enough period to have a significant impact on each teacher's practice. Furthermore, the approach also makes positive use on a regular basis of the support and insight of colleagues engaged in the same enterprise.

Making use of evidence-based classroom practice

There has been a huge increase in the number of sources of information drawing upon the research evidence for the effectiveness of different aspects of classroom practice (Marzano, 2003; Petty, 2006; Stronge, 2002; Thomas and Pring, 2004). These include copies of DfES research reports which are freely available at the DfES website (www.dfes.gov.uk) and a number of systematic reviews of research which are freely available at the Evidence for Policy and Practice Information and Coordinating Centre (EPPI-Centre) website (http://eppi.ioe.ac.uk). There are also numerous websites (e.g. www.teachernet.gov.uk; www.ttrb.ac.uk), presentations on *Teachers' TV*, and journals and magazines aimed at teachers in which a more accessible style of writing and/or presentation is used to present digests of research studies and their implications for classroom practice.

In addition, a number of initiatives have been funded which involve teachers doing research on their own practice as part of collaboration with other teachers working in the same topic area (e.g. academic acceleration for gifted pupils; the use of numeracy recovery programmes for pupils in Key Stage 2; the use of PowerPoint in drama lessons; the use of extended coursework projects in History in Key Stage 3). Several studies have indicated that such collaboration between teachers can have a very positive impact on the development of new skills and understanding about aspects of their classroom practice. A study by Erickson *et al.* (2005) found that collaborative projects involving teachers and teacher educators were particularly effective in enhancing the professional development of the teachers involved and improved the learning environment in these teachers' classrooms. They found that such collaborative work was effective because the work was embedded in the teachers' actual classroom practice; the teachers were able to share ideas in an atmosphere of trust; and the teachers also shared a precise mutual understanding of the issues involved in the aspects of the classroom practice they were considering.

There is now a wealth of information available to teachers, and attempts are being made to produce channels for this flow of information in which the information available can be vetted for quality and accuracy and highlighted in terms of its potential importance for classroom practice.

Teacher appraisal

Teacher appraisal, as part of a formal scheme operating at your school, should take place in a context where the aims of the scheme are explicitly stated in written guidelines issued to all staff, together with details of the procedures to be followed in carrying out, recording and reporting lesson observations. Such guidelines vary markedly from school to school, and certain details of the procedures may even operate differently to some extent within the same school, although they will need to be in line with the national framework for teacher appraisal in schools (Jones *et al.*, 2006; Middlewood and Cardno, 2001).

The stages of teacher appraisal

Teacher appraisal in schools involves four main stages:

- *A pre-appraisal stage.* In this stage, the 'appraisee' (the teacher being appraised) is asked to reflect on all aspects of their work as a teacher, including, in particular, their current classroom practice and areas of practice they may like to consider in detail or develop in some way. This stage is likely to involve the appraisee completing a questionnaire, which will include open-ended questions designed to encourage them to review and reflect on their current practice and identify any concerns they have.
- *Classroom observation.* This normally involves observation of two lessons. The selection of the lessons to be observed will be based on prior discussion about which lessons might be most appropriate for this, and about whether the appraiser could usefully focus on any particular aspects of the teaching.
- *An appraisal interview.* As part of this interview, the teacher's classroom practice is discussed, and any development needs in this respect are agreed and may form the basis of targets to be met during the subsequent development cycle.
- *Follow-up action.* If problems have been identified during the interview, action may need to be taken by the school to help resolve these. In addition, support of some kind may be required to help the appraisee to meet agreed development targets.

The role of the appraiser

One of the key tasks of the appraiser is to help a colleague reflect upon and develop their classroom teaching skills. This involves a number of important issues. First, the relationship between the appraiser and appraisee must be based on mutual trust and respect. The appraiser must have credibility with the appraisee and be seen as someone whose observations and comments will be valued. The appraisal process must also be collaborative (i.e. the appraiser and appraisee are jointly helping each other to make the process as valuable and as worthwhile as possible).

Second, the appraiser needs to be extremely careful and sensitive in how they communicate feedback to the appraisee. What is said must be scrupulously fair, and only judgemental in so far as the appraiser is raising an issue for discussion. The tone of the discussion should be one of equals comparing notes and views, and not one of the appraiser telling the appraisee how to teach better.

Third, it is essential that teachers being appraised feel they have ownership over the process. This means that the appraiser needs to help the appraisee reflect on their own practice and offer useful feedback to help them do so. Carrying out this role will require the appraiser to come to an understanding of the teacher's thoughts about their own teaching, their aims and intentions for a lesson, and their concerns about areas that might usefully be looked at in detail. The extent to which the appraiser is able to convey this may be limited by the nature of the scheme itself and how far its emphasis is clearly formative or summative. For example, some schemes have the tone of being a professional review, whilst others seem to have the tone of being more judgemental and inspectorial.

Recording the results of the appraisal

Part of the appraisal process requires that an agreed record of the appraisal be drawn up. At the very least this will be a written statement of what was agreed at the appraisal interview in terms of the teacher's current performance and development targets. At the other extreme, however, some documents have included a copy of the appraisee's initial self-review, the appraiser's comments on the lessons observed, and a summary of the areas and issues covered in the appraisal interview. In some schemes the observations of classroom teaching were recorded in the form of a profile. A typical profile comprises three elements together with a prompt list for each, as follows:

- *Preparation.* The activity was part of a properly planned programme; the aim of the activity was clear; a suitable approach was chosen from the options available; adequate and suitable resources were available; the learning environment had been considered.
- *Teaching skills.* The material was well presented; the pupils were actively involved; the teacher adapted the approach when necessary, was aware of individual needs within the group; and displayed mastery of the subject matter.
- *Follow-up.* Homework is set regularly (if appropriate); pupils' work is marked and recorded regularly; pupils receive appropriate feedback about their work; parents are informed of pupils' work and progress in accordance with school policy; the teacher evaluates the success of their teaching.

This teacher appraisal profile contains a space next to each of these three elements to record a summary of the discussion between the appraiser and appraisee. While a detailed listing of the major areas to be covered in an appraisal, together with their specific constituent elements, is helpful in indicating the aspects of teaching that may usefully receive attention, it becomes all too easy for the recording format to dictate what is looked at. As far as classroom teaching is concerned, the elements listed can take on a prescriptive quality and emphasise the summative aspect of appraisal. This will undermine the sense of ownership needed for the formative purpose to be encouraged. Fortunately, the experience of many teacher appraisal schemes indicates that a formative approach designed to encourage self-reflection and development has been widely employed (Jones *et al.*, 2006; Middlewood and Cardno, 2001).

Helping teachers to develop their classroom teaching skills

In helping colleagues to develop their classroom teaching skills, it is often essential to go beyond simply giving advice and guidance. The teachers may need a variety of experiences and support in order to develop in a particular way. Most significantly, they may benefit from observing colleagues in their own school or teachers in other schools, or by taking part in workshops and courses for experienced teachers aimed at developing specific skills and expertise.

Changes in teaching, learning and assessment practices in schools have major implications for in-service training and the provision of new resources. To expect teachers, for example, to be able to use the latest information technology packages, to prepare new coursework assessment activities, to adopt new investigational tasks, clearly requires major training support for those teachers who are not confident or do not have sufficient current expertise in such approaches. Appraisal must not simply identify such needs, but should also plan for how such needs can best be met.

Managing your time

There are few jobs that can compare with teaching for the variety of demands you have to deal with: lesson planning, classroom teaching, marking, administration, dealing with pupils' personal problems, school-based decision-making, setting examinations, meeting parents, collaborating with colleagues, carrying out managerial responsibilities, helping new members of staff and student teachers, and the purchase of resources and equipment, such as textbooks, machinery and materials. Being able to cope with such demands efficiently and effectively will have a bearing, directly or indirectly, on the quality of teaching and learning that takes place in your lessons.

Effective time management

You will need to develop skills that enable you to manage your time and effort to best effect. In addition, because of the changing nature of your work as a teacher as a result of your own career development and changes in teaching generally, you will need to review and reflect regularly upon how well you are doing this.

Time-management skills are essential if you are to manage your work and effort to best effect (Brown and Ralph, 1998; Neil and Morgan, 2003). Successful time management involves a number of important elements.

- *Be aware of your time*. You need to think about how much time you spend on particular demands, and decide whether this needs to be altered. For example, you may be spending too much time planning and preparing lessons to the point where you are 'gilding the lily'. Analysis may reveal that you could reduce planning time without any noticeable loss of quality. You may also be able to improve on the efficiency of your planning by, for example, making greater use of lesson plans given previously or by planning a course of lessons at the same time rather than individually.

- *Prioritise*. You have to decide in which order to undertake various tasks, taking account of their importance and urgency. The more important a task is, the more you should budget time to carry it out well in advance of the deadline, so that you do not have to do a rushed job under pressure at the last minute. If the task is urgent, you need to be flexible in postponing another task that can wait. In general, you should loosely try to meet demands in the order in which they confront you, but be able to prioritise urgent and important tasks as and when necessary.

- *Plan your time*. You need to think about planning your time in the short term (the school day), the medium term (the school week), and the long term (the academic term and year). Your planning for each time-frame ought to reflect your prioritising, so that by the end of each period the tasks with highest priority have been completed effectively, and those with lowest priority have been slotted in as and when appropriate. Advance planning is helpful in enabling you to prepare in good time and make necessary arrangements or take on other commitments in the light of such planning.

- *Match time to tasks*. Everyone has preferences about when and how they work most efficiently for given tasks. For example, some teachers may find that marking work late during a weekday evening is particularly productive, whilst others may find using some time immediately after the end of a school day works better. Organising your time so that you can undertake particular tasks at your most efficient time for each can help you develop regular routines that work well.

- *Deal with small tasks quickly*. There are a number of tasks that can be dealt with in a short period of time, either immediately or at an early opportunity. Getting such tasks done and out of the way as soon as possible helps to keep your desk clear. Leaving them for later often results in your finding you have several rather small tasks needing to be done that begin to clutter up your planning, and their delay in completion may start to cause inconvenience to yourself and others. However, be alert to the fact that some such tasks, although small, may require more considered and careful attention, which you may need to think through or on which you may need to consult others before acting.

- *Do not procrastinate.* Once you have recognised that there is a task to be done, try to plan when you are going to carry it out, and then do so at that time. Much time can be wasted by thinking about starting a task on several occasions and each time deciding to leave it for no good reason, or because it involves some unpleasantness that you are inclined to put off.
- *Be realistic.* You need to set yourself realistic demands, which means deciding what quality of work you can achieve in the time available. You may be trying to achieve a much higher quality than is really required, or carrying out a task much sooner than is sensible. Try not to accept unrealistic deadlines from others, as often such deadlines can easily be made more realistic.
- *Be able to say 'no'.* Some teachers always say 'yes' when asked to undertake various tasks, and this can easily result in them becoming overloaded, and being the first to be approached when a new task needs to be allocated. Saying 'no' occasionally provides others with feedback about how busy you may be and whether or not you feel the task is something you could usefully take on at the moment (this will help others in the school decide how best to manage the allocation of tasks to staff as a whole).
- *Delegate.* There are many tasks you can appropriately ask a colleague or a pupil to undertake and, from time to time, you should review whether some of the tasks you carry out should be delegated. For example, you could easily find yourself spending a whole day, off and on, trying to find out something about a pupil's circumstances that a colleague was better placed to have found out in just a few minutes. You may also be spending too much time on routine tasks, such as handing out books, equipment, worksheets, collecting marks and checking progress, in ways that can be better done by asking pupils to carry out some of these tasks.

As well as developing time management skills yourself, you should also be helping others to do so. For example, you should help pupils become aware of how to organise and pace their efforts in meeting deadlines within a lesson or over a longer period. In your dealings with colleagues, you can also help them to plan how tasks that affect you and others need to be organised so that appropriate deadlines and task allocations are set; for example, planning that pupils do not have too many coursework deadlines falling on the same date, or that time to mark examination work does not coincide unnecessarily with other busy periods in the school.

Time-management skills are not a panacea that will alleviate all time pressures on you. Nevertheless, they do have a major impact on keeping avoidable pressures to a minimum, and helping you to maintain a high quality of performance in how you undertake the variety of tasks facing you. Indeed, they are one of the important sets of skills a new teacher needs to develop in the early years of teaching, and then needs to develop further as the teacher's role and commitments in school alter.

Dealing with stress

When teachers feel angry, depressed, anxious, nervous, frustrated or tense as a result of some aspect of their work as teachers, this is referred to as 'teacher stress'. Teacher stress has been widely discussed and researched for many years, and it appears that most teachers experience some stress from time to time, and that a sizeable number of teachers – about one in four – experience a great deal of stress fairly often (Hayes, C. 2006; Kyriacou, 2000). Being able to deal with the demands of teaching so that sources of stress are minimised or dealt with effectively is another important set of skills needed by teachers.

Sources of teacher stress

The main sources of stress facing teachers fall into ten areas:

- teaching pupils who lack motivation
- maintaining discipline
- time pressures and workload
- coping with change
- being evaluated by others
- dealing with colleagues
- self-esteem and status
- administration and management
- role conflict and ambiguity
- poor working conditions.

How stress is triggered

The particular sources of stress experienced by individual teachers vary greatly from teacher to teacher. However, what appears to be central to the experience of stress is that it is triggered by the teacher's perception that the demands made on them threaten their self-esteem or well-being in some way.

As a teacher, there are a whole host of demands that have to be dealt with, including disciplining pupils, getting marking done in time, explaining a pupil's poor progress to their parents, finding that equipment needed for a lesson is out of order. Any one of these situations has the potential to lead to the experience of stress. What seems to be crucial, however, is that two conditions are evident:

- The teacher feels that meeting the demands made is important (i.e. failure to meet the demands successfully may have undesirable consequences).
- The teacher feels that meeting these demands successfully will be difficult or impossible to achieve in the particular circumstances.

As a result of these two conditions, the teacher views the situation facing them as threatening, and that immediately triggers the experience of stress. If, however, the teacher does not view the demands as important or feels that they can easily meet the demands, then no threat is perceived, and hence no stress is triggered. For example, if in the middle of a lesson a pupil is rude to you, in a split second you may judge that you are not sure how to deal with the situation, and begin to feel nervous and anxious, particularly if you feel the situation may escalate. Furthermore, if you feel that by failing to deal with the situation you may be seen by pupils, colleagues, or yourself, as having inadequate skills in class control, this will threaten your self-esteem. Your feelings may be particularly strong if you regard the remark as an intolerable insult, which embarrasses you in front of the whole class. In such circumstances you will experience stress. In contrast, if you judge the situation as one you can deal with quite easily, and perhaps even as a rather trivial incident of little consequence, you will experience no stress.

Thus the reason why demands that cause a great deal of stress to one teacher may cause little stress to another teacher, lies simply in how the two teachers perceive the situation differently in terms of its importance and their ability to deal with it.

The impact of stress on your teaching

Teacher stress may undermine the quality of your teaching in two main ways. First, if you find teaching stressful over a long period, it may start to undermine your satisfaction with the work, and may lead to you becoming disaffected with teaching. This is likely to have some impact on the time and effort you are prepared to give to the quality of your teaching. Second, when you experience stress, this can undermine the quality of your interaction with pupils in the classroom. Effective teaching very much depends on a positive classroom climate, and, in particular, on a good rapport with pupils, coupled with supporting and encouraging pupils' efforts. When you experience stress, that generosity of spirit towards pupils, which contributes to a positive classroom climate, can disappear, and you may react to problems and difficulties in a less well tempered or, even worse, in an openly hostile manner. Therefore being able to deal effectively with stress will help you to maintain a high quality of teaching.

Coping strategies

Dealing with stress successfully involves using two types of coping strategy: direct action techniques and palliative techniques. In *direct action techniques,* you need to identify what is causing you stress and why, and then decide on a course of action that will deal successfully with that source of stress.

For example, if a particular pupil is disruptive almost every lesson, you may try a new strategy to deal with this. If you feel friction has developed between you and a colleague, you may try to re-establish a good relationship by being overtly more sociable and friendly towards your colleague. If you find that you are not able to mark pupils' work in good time, you may use some time-management strategies to budget your time differently. As well as taking action on your own initiative, you can also usefully consult with colleagues to see if certain problems are common to them, or whether action involving colleagues can help deal with the source of stress. The use of direct action techniques to deal with sources of stress may lead to immediate success, or may involve long-term action, particularly if successful action depends on you improving certain skills.

Take time to relax and unwind after work

However, there are some sources of stress that you will not be able to deal with successfully by direct action techniques, and here you will need to use *palliative techniques*. Palliative techniques are things you can do to relieve the experience of stress, even when the source of stress persists. Particularly useful are mental techniques, such as getting things in perspective, trying to see the humour in a situation, trying to detach yourself from personal and emotional involvement in a situation, and sharing your worries and concerns with others. In addition, physical techniques, such as trying to relax whenever possible, or having a coffee or a bar of chocolate during break time, are useful. Some teachers have developed useful physical techniques based on relaxation exercises that can help them to keep calm and relaxed in a stressful situation. Being able to relax and unwind after work is also very important.

Developing your own approach to coping with stress

In general, direct action techniques should always be tried to deal with a particular source of stress before palliative techniques are used, since if the former are successful, the source of stress is dealt with rather than simply accommodated. Your approach to stress, however, needs to be tailored to your circumstances and personality. For example, while for one teacher more preparation time at home would be helpful, for another more time spent at home relaxing would be better. Nevertheless, the following advice is generally useful:

- Identify and deal with problems as soon as possible.
- Develop skills and procedures to help you deal with the demands on you, particularly organisational and time-management skills.
- See whether some sources of stress are partly of your own making, such as avoidable confrontations with pupils or colleagues, or accepting tasks that are too taxing.
- Keep things in perspective, and try to form realistic expectations about your own performance and that of others.
- Share your worries and concerns with others.
- Maintain a balance between your work as a teacher and your life outside school (a healthy and enjoyable life outside school will enhance your self-esteem and the inner strength you have to deal with problems at school).

It is also important to note that teachers collectively can do much to mitigate stress by establishing a supportive climate in the school to help each other overcome difficulties, and by ensuring that demands on teachers are organised and allocated in a way that does not create stress which could have been avoided, such as allocating too many important tasks to the same member of staff, or fixing important deadlines too near to each other.

Further reading

Bubb, S. (2004) *The Insider's Guide to Early Professional Development: Succeed in Your First Five Years as a Teacher.* London: RoutledgeFalmer. This book includes a good overview of the areas where beginning teachers need to develop their understanding and skills.

Jacklin, A., Griffiths, V. and Robinson, C. (2006) *Beginning Primary Teaching: Moving Beyond Survival.* Maidenhead: Open University Press. A very good analysis of the areas of professional development, including the skills involved in improving classroom practice, for primary school teachers.

Leach, S. (2006) *How to be a Successful Secondary Teacher.* London: Continuum. An insightful and well-informed guide to the areas of professional development for beginning secondary school teachers.

Petty, G. (2006) *Evidence-Based Teaching: A Practical Approach.* Cheltenham: Nelson Thornes. An excellent analysis of effective teaching which draws upon research evidence concerning the effectiveness of different teaching methods.

Key questions about your reflection and evaluation

1 Do I regularly consider my current practice with a view to identifying aspects that can be usefully developed?
2 Do I make adequate use of evaluating my lessons in informing my future planning and practice?

3 Do I make use of systematic methods of collecting data about my current practice that may be helpful?
4 Do I try to keep well-informed about developments in teaching, learning and assessment in schools that have implications for my teaching?
5 Do I make use of a variety of different ways of developing a particular teaching skill (i.e. attending workshops, using training manuals, collaborating with colleagues)?
6 Do I make the best use of my involvement in a scheme of teacher appraisal to consider my development needs?
7 How well do I help colleagues to appraise and develop their classroom practice?
8 Do I regularly review how I can organise my time and effort to better effect?
9 Do I use a range of useful strategies and techniques to deal with sources of stress effectively?
10 Do I help create a supportive climate in my school to help colleagues discuss and overcome problems?

Bibliography

Avramidis, E. (2006) 'Promoting inclusive education: from "expertism" to sustainable inclusive practices'. In Webb, R. (ed.) *Changing Teaching and Learning in the Primary School* (pp. 103–114). Maidenhead: Open University Press.

Berliner, D. (1995) 'Teacher expertise'. In Anderson, L. W. (ed.) *International Encyclopaedia of Teaching and Teacher Education*, 2nd edn (pp. 46–51). Oxford: Pergamon.

Black, P., Harrison, C., Lee, C., Marshall, B. and Wiliam, D. (2003) *Assessment for Learning: Putting it into Practice*. Maidenhead: Open University Press.

Borich, G. D. (2007) *Effective Teaching Methods: Research Based Practice*, 6th edn. Englewood Cliffs: Prentice Hall.

Briggs, M., Woodfield, A., Martin, C. and Swatton, P. (2003) *Assessment for Learning and Teaching in Primary Schools*. Exeter: Learning Matters.

British Educational Communications and Technology Agency (2005) *Becta's View: Personalising Learning with ICT*. Coventry: Becta.

Brophy, J. E. (2004) *Motivating Students to Learn*, 2nd edn. New York: Lawrence Erlbaum.

Brown, M. and Ralph, S. (1998) *Time Management for Teachers: A Practical Guide to Effective Strategies and Techniques*. Plymouth: Northcote House.

Bubb, S. (2004) *The Insider's Guide to Early Professional Development: Succeed in Your First Five Years as a Teacher*. London: RoutledgeFalmer.

Butt, G. (2006) *Lesson Planning*, 2nd edn. London: Kogan Page.

Campbell, J., Kyriakides, L., Muijs, D. and Robinson, W. (2004) *Assessing Teacher Effectiveness: Developing a Differentiated Model*. London: RoutledgeFalmer.

Chaplain, R. (2003) *Teaching Without Disruption in the Primary School: A Model for Managing Pupil Behaviour*. London: RoutledgeFalmer.

Cheminais, R. (2006) *Every Child Matters: A Practical Guide for Teachers*. London: David Fulton.

Clarke, S. (2005) *Formative Assessment in Action: Weaving the Elements Together*. London: Hodder Murray.

Cohen, L., Manion, L. and Morrison, K. (2004) *A Guide to Teaching Practice*, 5th edn. London: RoutledgeFalmer.

Costello, P. (2003) *Action Research*. London: Continuum.

Cullingford, C. (2003) *The Best Years of their Lives? Pupils' Experiences of School*. London: RoutledgeFalmer.

Day, C. (2004) *A Passion for Teaching*. London: RoutledgeFalmer.

Day, C., Stobart, G., Sammons, P., Kington, A., Gu, Q., Smees, R. and Mujtaba, T. (2006) *Variations in Teachers' Work, Lives and Effectiveness (Research Report RR743)*. London: DfES.

Day, C., Sammons, P., Stobart, G., Kington, A. and Gu, Q. (2007) *Teachers Matter: Connecting Lives, Work and Effectiveness*. Maidenhead: Open University Press.

Dean, J. (2000) *Improving Children's Learning: Effective Teaching in the Primary School*. London: Routledge.

Department for Education and Skills (2003a) *Key Stage 3 National Strategy Key Messages: Pedagogy and Practice*. London: DfES.

Department for Education and Skills (2003b) *Excellence and Enjoyment: A Strategy for Primary Schools*. London: DfES.

Department for Education and Skills (2004a) *Pedagogy and Practice: Teaching and Learning in Secondary Schools*. London: DfES.

Department for Education and Skills (2004b) *Every Child Matters: Change for Children in Schools*. London: DfES.

Department for Education and Skills (2004c) *A National Conversation about Personalised Learning*. London: DfES.

Department for Education and Skills (2005a) *Key Stage 3 National Strategy. Leading in Learning: Developing Thinking Skills at Key Stage 3. Handbook for Teachers*. London: DfES.

Department for Education and Skills (2005b) *Higher Standards, Better Schools for All: More Choice for Parents and Pupils* (White Paper, cm 6677). London: Stationery Office.

Erickson, G., Brandes, G. M., Mitchell, I. and Mitchell, J. (2005) 'Collaborative teacher learning: findings from two professional development projects'. *Teaching and Teacher Education*, vol. 21 (7), pp. 787–798.

Evertson, C. M. and Weinstein, C. S. (eds) (2006) *Handbook of Classroom Management: Research, Practice, and Contemporary Issues*. Mahwah, New Jersey: Lawrence Erlbaum.

Fraser, B. J. (2002) 'Learning environments research: yesterday, today and tomorrow'. In Goh, S. C. and Khine, M. S. (eds) *Studies in Educational Learning Environments: An International Perspective* (pp. 1–27). Singapore: World Scientific.

Gardner, J. (ed.) (2006) *Assessment and Learning*. London: Sage.

Gillespie, H. (2006) *Unlocking Learning and Teaching with ICT: Identifying and Overcoming Barriers*. London: David Fulton.

Gillies, R. M. (2004) 'The effects of cooperative activities on junior high school students during small group learning'. *Learning and Instruction*, vol. 14 (2), pp. 197–213.

Gronlund, N. E. T. and Nivaldo, J. (2004) *Writing Instructional Objectives for Teaching and Assessment*, 7th edn. Englewood Cliffs: Prentice Hall.

Hargreaves, D. H. (1982) *The Challenge for the Comprehensive School: Culture, Curriculum and Community*. London: Routledge and Kegan Paul.

Hay McBer (2000) *Research into Teacher Effectiveness: A Model of Teacher Effectiveness (Research Report RR216)*. London: DfEE.

Haydn, T. (2007) *Managing Pupil Behaviour: Key Issues in Teaching and Learning.* London: Routledge.

Hayes, C. (2006) *Stress Relief for Teachers: The 'Coping' Triangle.* London: Routledge.

Hayes, D. (2006) *The Art of Interactive Teaching.* Exeter: Learning Matters.

Hobson, A. J., Malderez, A., Tracey, L., Giannakaki, M. S., Pell, R. G., Kerr, K., Chambers, G. N., Tomlinson, P. D. and Roper, T. (2006) *Becoming a Teacher: Student Teachers' Experiences of Initial Teacher Training in England (Research Report RR744).* London: DfES.

Ireson, J. and Hallam, S. (2002) *Ability Grouping in Education.* London: Paul Chapman.

Jacklin, A., Griffiths, V. and Robinson, C. (2006) *Beginning Primary Teaching: Moving Beyond Survival.* Maidenhead: Open University Press.

Jaques, D. (2000) *Learning in Groups: A Handbook for Improving Group Work,* 3rd edn. London: RoutledgeFalmer.

Jones, J., Jenkin, M. and Lord, S. (2006) *Developing Effective Teacher Performance.* London: Paul Chapman.

Kaplan, A., Gheen, M. and Midgley, C. (2002) 'Classroom goal structure and student disruptive behaviour'. *British Journal of Educational Psychology,* vol. 72 (2), pp. 191–211.

Kerry, T. (2002) *Explaining and Questioning.* Cheltenham: Nelson Thornes.

Kerry, T. and Wilding, M. (2004) *Effective Classroom Teacher: Developing the Skills You Need in Today's Classroom.* London: Pearson.

Koshy, V. (2005) *Action Research for Improving Practice: A Practical Guide.* London: Paul Chapman.

Kounin, J. S. (1970) *Discipline and Group Management in Classrooms.* New York: Holt, Rinehart and Winston.

Kutnick, P., Sebba, J., Blatchford, P., Galton, M. and Thorp, J. (with MacIntyre, H. and Berdondini, L.) (2005) *The Effects of Pupil Grouping: Literature Review (Research Report RR688).* London: DfES.

Kyriacou, C. (1997) *Effective Teaching in Schools,* 2nd edn. Cheltenham: Nelson Thornes.

Kyriacou, C. (2000) *Stress-busting for Teachers.* Cheltenham: Nelson Thornes.

Kyriacou, C. (2003) *Helping Troubled Pupils.* Cheltenham: Nelson Thornes.

Kyriacou, C. (2005) 'The impact of daily mathematics lessons in England on pupil confidence and competence in early mathematics: a systematic review'. *British Journal of Educational Studies,* vol. 53 (2), pp. 168–186.

Kyriacou, C. and Cheng, H. (1993) 'Student teachers' attitudes towards the humanistic approach to teaching and learning in schools'. *European Journal of Teacher Education,* vol. 16, pp. 163–168.

Kyriacou, C. and Kunc, R. (2007) 'Beginning teachers' expectations of teaching'. *Teaching and Teacher Education.* Accepted for publication.

Kyriacou, C. and McKelvey, J. (1985) 'An exploration of individual differences in "effective" teaching'. *Educational Review,* vol. 37 (1), pp. 13–17.

Kyriacou, C., Avramidis, E., Benmansour, N., Hoie, H., Hultgren, A., Kennedy, D., Ortega, J., Stephens, P. and Tabuchi, I. (2007) 'An international comparison of student teachers' views of pupil misbehaviour in six settings'. Manuscript in preparation.

Leach, S. (2006) *How to be a Successful Secondary Teacher*. London: Continuum.

Leask, M. and Pachler, N. (eds) (2005) *Learning to Teach using ICT in the Secondary School: A Companion to School Experience*, 2nd edn. London: Routledge.

Lewis, A. and Norwich, B. (eds) (2005) *Special Teaching for Special Children?: Pedagogies for Inclusion*. Maidenhead: Open University Press.

MacBeath, J. (2006) *School Inspection and Self-Evaluation: Working with the New Relationship*. London: Routledge.

Marzano, R. J. (2003) *What Works in Schools: Translating Research into Action*. Alexandria, Virginia: Association for Supervision and Curriculum Development.

Maslow, A. H. (1987) *Motivation and Personality,* 3rd edn. New York: Harper Collins.

McCormick, J. and Leask, M. (2005) 'Teaching styles'. In Capel, S., Leask, M. and Turner, T. (eds) (2005) *Learning to Teach in the Secondary School: A Companion to School Experience,* 4th edn (pp. 276–291). London: Routledge.

McCutcheon, G. and Milner, H. R. (2002) 'A contemporary study of teacher planning in a high school English class'. *Teachers and Teaching: Theory and Practice,* vol. 8 (1), pp. 81–94.

McNamara, E. (2001) *Positive Pupil Management and Motivation*. London: David Fulton.

McNeil, F. and Sammons, P. (2006) *Improving Schools,* 2nd edn. London: RoutledgeFalmer.

Middlewood, D. and Cardno, C. E. M. (eds) (2001) *Managing Teacher Appraisal and Performance*. London: RoutledgeFalmer.

Moyles, J., Merry, R., Paterson, F. and Esarte-Sarries, V. (2003) *Interactive Teaching in the Primary School: Digging Deeper into Meanings.* Maidenhead: Open University Press.

Muijs, D. and Reynolds, D. (2005) *Effective Teaching: Evidence and Practice,* 2nd edn. London: Sage.

Myhill, D., Jones, S. and Hopper, R. (2006) *Talking, Listening, Learning: Effective Talk in the Primary Classroom*. Maidenhead: Open University Press.

Neil, P. and Morgan, C. (2003) *Continuing Professional Development for Teachers: From Induction to Senior Management*. London: Kogan Page.

O'Donnell, A. M., Reeve, J. and Smith, J. K. (2007) *Educational Psychology: Reflection for Action*. New York: Wiley.

Ofsted (1995) *The Ofsted Handbook: Guidance and Resource Packs for the Inspection of Schools*. London: HMSO.

Ofsted (2002) *Good Teaching, Effective Departments: Findings from a HMI Survey of Subject Teaching in Secondary Schools, 2000/2001 (HMI Report 337)*. London: Ofsted.

Ofsted (2006) *The Annual Report of Her Majesty's Chief Inspector of Schools 2005/2006*. London: The Stationery Office.

Opdenakker, M.-C. and Van Damme, J. (2006) 'Teacher characteristics and teaching styles as effectiveness enhancing factors of classroom practice'. *Teaching and Teacher Education,* vol. 22 (1), pp. 1–21.

Perrott, E. (1982) *Effective Teaching.* London: Longman.

Petty, G. (2006) *Evidence-Based Teaching: A Practical Approach.* Cheltenham: Nelson Thornes.

Pollard, A. and James, M. (eds) (2004) *Personalised Learning: A Commentary by the Teaching and Learning Research Programme.* Swindon: ESRC.

Pollard, A. and Triggs, P. with Broadfoot, P., McNess, E. and Osborn, M. (2000) *What Pupils Say: Changing Policy and Practice in Primary Education.* London: Continuum.

Pollard, A. with Collins, J., Maddock, M., Simco, N., Swaffield, S., Warin, J. and Warwick, P. (2005) *Reflective Teaching,* 2nd edn. London: Continuum.

Porter, L. (2000) *Behaviour in Schools.* Maidenhead: Open University Press.

Postholm, M. B. (2006) 'Assessment during project work'. *Teaching and Teacher Education,* vol. 22 (2), pp. 150–163.

Pritchard, A. (2005) *Ways of Learning: Learning Theories and Learning Styles in the Classroom.* London: David Fulton.

Pye, J. (1988) *Invisible Children.* Oxford: Oxford University Press.

Robins, A. (2006) *Mentoring in the Early Years.* London: Paul Chapman.

Rogers, B. (1998) *You Know the Fair Rule: Strategies for Making the Hard Job of Discipline and Behaviour Management in School Easier,* 2nd edn. London: Prentice Hall.

Rogers, B. (2006) *Classroom Behaviour: A Practical Guide to Effective Teaching, Behaviour Management and Colleague Support,* 2nd edn. London: Paul Chapman.

Rogers, C. R. and Freiberg, H. J. (1994) *Freedom to Learn*, 3rd edn. New York: Merrill.

Seidel, T., Rimmele, R. and Prenzel, M. (2005) 'Clarity and coherence of lesson goals as a scaffold for student learning'. *Learning and Instruction,* vol. 15 (6), pp. 539–556.

Shulman, L. S. (1987) 'Knowledge and teaching: foundations of the new reform'. *Harvard Educational Review*, vol. 57 (1), pp. 1–22.

Skowron, J. (2006) *Powerful Lesson Planning: Every Teacher's Guide to Effective Instruction,* 2nd edn. London: Sage.

Smith., C. J. and Laslett, R. (1992) *Effective Classroom Management: A Teacher's Guide*, 2nd edn. London: Routledge.

Smith, E. and Gorard, S. (2005) ' "They don't give us our marks": the role of formative feedback in student progress'. *Assessment in Education,* vol. 12 (1), pp. 21–38.

Smith, F., Hardman, F., Wall, K. and Mroz, M. (2004) 'Interactive whole class teaching in the National Literacy and Numeracy Strategies'. *British Educational Research Journal,* vol. 30 (3), pp. 395–411.

Smith, F., Hardman, F. and Higgins, S. (2006) 'The impact of interactive whiteboards on teacher–pupil interaction in the National Literacy and Numeracy Strategies'. *British Educational Research Journal,* vol. 32 (3), pp. 443–457.

Smith, I. (2005) *Different in Similar Ways: Making Sense of Learning Styles*. London: Stationery Office.

Steer, A. (chair) (2005) *Learning Behaviour: The Report of the Practitioners' Group on School Behaviour and Discipline (the Steer Report)*. London: DfES.

Stephens, P. (1996) *Essential Mentoring Skills*. Cheltenham: Nelson Thornes.

Stephens, P. and Crawley, T. (1994) *Becoming an Effective Teacher*. Cheltenham: Nelson Thornes.

Stronge, J. H. (2002) *Qualities of Effective Teachers*. Alexandria, Virginia: Association for Supervision and Curriculum Development.

Tanner, H. (2003) *Marking and Assessment*. London: Continuum.

Thomas, G. and Pring, R. (eds) (2004) *Evidence-based Practice in Education*. Maidenhead: Open University Press.

Tileston, D. W. (2004) *What Every Teacher Should Know About Instructional Planning*. London: Corwin.

Training and Development Agency for Schools (2007) *Professional Standards for Teachers from September 2007*. www.tda.gov.uk.

Van Der Valk, T. and Broekman, H. (1999) 'The lesson preparation method: a way investigating pre-service teachers' pedagogical content knowledge'. *European Journal of Teacher Education,* vol. 22 (1), pp. 11–22.

Walsh, J. A. and Settes, B. D. (2005) *Quality Questioning: Research-based Practice to Engage Every Learner*. London: Sage.

Watkins, C. (2005) *Classrooms as Learning Communities: What's in it for Schools?* London: RoutledgeFalmer.

Webb, R. (2006) 'Teachers' perspectives on teaching and learning in a performativity culture'. In Webb, R. (ed.) *Changing Teaching and Learning in the Primary School*. (pp. 33–46). Maidenhead: Open University Press.

Weeden, P., Winter, J. and Broadfoot, P. (2002) *Assessment: What's in it for Schools?* London: RoutledgeFalmer.

Wheeler, S. (ed.) (2005) *Transforming Primary ICT*. Exeter: Learning Matters.

Wragg, E. C. (2005) *The Art and Science of Teaching and Learning: The Selected Works of Ted Wragg*. London: RoutledgeFalmer.

Wragg, E. C. and Brown, G. (2001a) *Explaining in the Primary School,* 2nd edn. London: RoutledgeFalmer.

Wragg, E. C. and Brown, G. (2001b) *Explaining in the Secondary School,* 2nd edn. London: RoutledgeFalmer.

Wragg, E. C. and Brown, G. (2001c) *Questioning in the Primary School,* 2nd edn. London: RoutledgeFalmer.

Wragg, E. C. and Brown, G. (2001d) *Questioning in the Secondary School,* 2nd edn. London: RoutledgeFalmer.

Author index

Subject index